Teaching Life Skills at the Library

Teaching Life Skills at the Library

Programs and Activities on Money Management, Career Development, and More

KIMBERLI S. BUCKLEY

CHICAGO 2022

Kimberli S. Buckley has over fifteen years of experience in the library field working with teens and adults. She is currently the library manager at Concord Library in Contra Costa County, California. Kimberli has a passion for teaching classes on life skills for emerging adults. She teaches at San Jose State University's School of Information and also teaches an online class called Growing Up Is Hard. She loves to be creative when it comes to library programming, and she has been known to tap into her inner unicorn to bring all her ideas to life. Kimberli has an MLIS degree from San Jose State University and an MA in consciousness studies from John F. Kennedy University.

Extensive effort has gone into ensuring the reliability of the information in this book; however, the publisher makes no warranty, express or implied, with respect to the material contained herein.

ISBN: 978-0-8389-4890-3 (paper)

Library of Congress Cataloging-in-Publication Data

Names: Buckley, Kimberli S., 1965- author.
Title: Teaching life skills at the library : programs and activities on money management, career development, and more / Kimberli S. Buckley.
Description: Chicago : ALA Editions, 2022. | Includes bibliographical references and index. | Summary: "This book provides easy-to-implement activities that readers can use to develop life skills classes at their library"—Provided by publisher.
Identifiers: LCCN 2022003269 | ISBN 9780838948903 (paperback)
Subjects: LCSH: Libraries—Activity programs. | Life skills—Study and teaching—Activity programs.
Classification: LCC Z716.33 .B83 2022 | DDC 025.5—dc23/eng/20220422
LC record available at https://lccn.loc.gov/2022003269

Book design by Kim Hudgins in the Aleo, Gotham, and Quinn Text typefaces.

♾ This paper meets the requirements of ANSI/NISO Z39.48-1992 (Permanence of Paper).

Printed in the United States of America
26 25 24 23 22   5 4 3 2 1

Contents

Preface | vii

Acknowledgments | xiii

Introduction: You've Got This! | xv

PART I PLANNING LIFE SKILLS PROGRAMS

1 Let's Start Planning 3

2 Partnership Opportunities and Program Promotions 11

3 Evaluate and Sustain Your Life Skills Programs 17

PART II LIFE SKILLS ACTIVITY PLANS

4 Jobs 23

5 Money 31

6 Cooking 39

7 Self-Care 47

8 Personal Care 55

9 Home Skills 63

10 Communication 71

11 Relationships with Friends and Family 79

12 Stress Management 87

Conclusion: Taking Care of Business | 95

Appendixes

  Appendix A: Planning Template for a Life Skills Program | 97

  Appendix B: Reading Tie-Ins | 101

Index | 111

Preface

It takes courage to grow up and become who you really are.

—E. E. CUMMINGS

MY BACKGROUND IN TEACHING LIFE SKILLS HAS BEEN A JOURNEY THROUGH working in both school and public libraries, raising my own kids, and my own personal transformation. I first became interested in teaching life skills in 2014. I had been a teen librarian for many years, and I was embarking on a new journey and had just become a new library manager. I was managing two libraries in a community that was socioeconomically disadvantaged. This community wasn't just affected by a lower income status, but by lower educational opportunities, and the community members also suffered from a lower quality of life in specific neighborhoods.

Shortly after I started managing, I was contacted by a local high-school teacher who told me that she had a group of seniors who were going to be graduating soon. She told me that they could benefit from some life skills classes before they graduated. She asked me if I could come up with a variety of topics and teach life skills classes for her students. This sounded like a great opportunity for me to create a partnership with this teacher and the school, so I took on this challenge with high hopes. I did have some reservations, though. I wondered if I could pull it off. I am a grown-up, of course, but I'm not an expert on how to be one. Seriously, my favorite colors are pink and purple, I love unicorns, and throwing glitter is my superpower. In all seriousness though, it was really enlightening to brainstorm about the topics that I could teach these students.

The one question I had going through my mind was: how am I going to come up with life skills topics and teach students so that they want to learn these topics? I thought about my background and how I had graduated with a master's degree in consciousness studies and holistic health long before I was a librarian. Completing this degree was an incredible experience for me, and I really wanted to bring what I had learned through consciousness studies into my life skills classes because my studies had been drawn from psychology, philosophy, sociology, art, and holistic practices like guided therapy and dream studies. I've been asked many times what the heck consciousness studies is. In essence, the focus is on the transformative experiences, practices, and beliefs of many cultural, spiritual, and psychotherapeutic traditions. Through this graduate program I was taken on a journey of self-discovery and transformation. The program is designed not only to galvanize your wisdom, courage, love, joy, and vitality, but also to enrich your sense of meaning, passion, and purpose. It was then that I realized that I've been through a lot in my life; and with the knowledge I had from my consciousness studies degree, I was sure that I could come up with a list of the most important topics and create some really amazing life skills classes and programs. It's true that life skills are important, and most of the time these skills are learned through life experiences, so I knew I was ready to start on a new journey of teaching and sharing my wisdom.

During the research and planning process, I also realized that anyone at any age could benefit from a life skills program. Most life skills programs are geared to help individuals so that they can effectively manage the daily obstacles in life. At that same time, it just so happened that my son was turning eighteen, and he gave me a lot of ideas on topics. He told me that he was disappointed that he hadn't learned any basic life skills in school. He mentioned that he was interested in learning how to apply to colleges, find a job, and acquire cooking skills. With all of the questions that he had, it felt like the perfect time for me to come up with a comprehensive list of important life skills topics and programs that would be ideal for any person to learn.

The life skills classes I designed went over well, and I ended up planning and presenting programs at the library for the next several years. I also passed a lot of the information on to my son. It was sort of interesting when several years later the term adulting came into play, because it seems that many people were using this term as a way to mock the younger generation. This made me a little sad because it is my son's generation that is being targeted as not being ready for adulthood, but I knew from his responses that he wasn't learning any life skills in school that he needed to know in order to properly become an adult.

This rings true for many people who are struggling to learn how to take care of themselves; and it's true that there is usually a point in each of our lives when we will need to become more independent and start to take better care of ourselves. But . . . what if we are unequipped to handle the curveballs that life throws at us? This can easily happen to any one of us and if it does, there are some crucial things that we will need to learn before we can take steps to living on our own.

What are these steps and how do we get there? It's all about learning life skills. If you've heard of the term life skills, then you know that these are the skills that everyone needs to know in order to become independent. The great thing is that a program at the library that focuses on different life skills can be useful for any age group and can be very meaningful for those who need a little guidance in this area.

I've also heard many people say that they just don't want to "be an adult" anymore, as if they actually have a choice to be an adult . . . or not. Many people don't like the term adulting because it suggests a negative outlook on individuals who don't really want to grow up or who detest doing adult things. This connects to the term life skills because these are the skills and accomplishments that we all have to learn in order to sustain ourselves, and we can really look at this as a positive thing that we can all do for ourselves.

What I have learned after teaching life skills programs for the past several years is that many people are looking for ways to learn how to successfully take care of themselves, but they just don't know where to go to get the help. If we look back over the last one hundred years, we can see that people grew up and took on the role of becoming an adult in a very different way than today. Today, many people don't know how to seek out responsibilities as an accomplishment, and this could become a pitfall for the younger generation now. We really don't want anyone avoiding their responsibilities, and many are doing this by staying within the comforts they know—instead of stepping into unknown territory and learning the life skills needed to evolve into maturity, which is actually a rite of passage that involves growth and transformation.

The way that people grow and develop is essential to how they are going to live their lives as grown-ups. If we look even deeper, we can discover why life skills are important and why we need them. Life skills are needed to transition through life's milestones, such as moving out on your own, going to college or getting a job, getting in a serious relationship, or getting married, and sometimes even becoming a parent, if that path is chosen.

Some might say that reaching milestones doesn't really define a person's status as responsible, and that is a good point. Life skills are more about learning the ordinary, day-to-day responsibilities that you may have to take on, and this is done by imparting knowledge through education. Other abilities like independent thinking and self-reliance are also necessary for surviving on your own, but these usually come through one's own life experiences and personal growth over time.

There is no magical milestone marking when a person will become responsible. Some of the accomplishments that are supported by life skills might be going to college, supporting oneself financially, living with a roommate, becoming self-sufficient, and contributing to a household. Ultimately, life skills programs help prepare us to live on our own and to become responsible beings.

We all need opportunities to learn things for our own personal survival, but sometimes those opportunities don't always come up if we live in certain environments. This is an area where the library can step in and fulfill a component of lifelong learning, which can help us in both our coping skills and our personal development.

Many people might think that learning about life skills is boring, or wonder why anyone cares about that stuff, but these are very important tasks that bridge the gap between living as a dependent and venturing out on your own. It's like acknowledging the gap between expectation, achievement, and reality. No matter how boring we think it is, growing up is hard, and the challenge is to embrace all the resources that are out there in order to narrow that gap and make it a little easier to cross.

For some people, age is just a number, and it doesn't signify what the person should have achieved by a certain age or time frame. Most people will graduate from high school around the age of eighteen, and then their life skills will gradually develop over time with experience and opportunities. Upon graduation, it could take five years or in some cases even ten years to mature or reach optimum adult status. The idea of not putting a number on your age has become more common today because schools often don't teach the basic life skills that people need to thrive as they move through the defining stages of their lives.

One last thing I want to let you know is that I have included an appendix at the end of the book called "Reading Tie-Ins." These are books that I highly recommend when you start to plan your own life skills programs at the library. I have carefully curated these titles and have used them myself in my life skills planning. They will be extremely helpful and will give you some great insights going forward. You don't have to purchase all of these books; they are reading suggestions, and you may find them right inside your own library.

Acknowledgments

I'VE BEEN ON A LONG JOURNEY DISCOVERING AND LEARNING ABOUT THE essential life skills that one needs to survive as an adult. After many years of immersing myself and learning all about life skills, I feel that I have come to acquire some very precious knowledge. My goal now is to share this knowledge with everyone. I have a deeper understanding of what it means to grow up in today's world and how difficult it can be to start out on your own. I have had many mentors who have brought me to this realization. I would like to dedicate this book to all of those mentors and thank them from the bottom of my heart for inspiring me to do the work that I do.

Immense gratitude goes out to my mother, who has encouraged me as well as surprised me with her intellect and intuition. Some might say that the two of us grew up together. She also knows things about me that I don't even know about my own self. Her unconditional love is what propels me through life.

Many thanks to Myles Buckley, my supreme guide in life, my best friend, and my husband. He has taught me to reach for the stars and achieve my dreams. He knew I could complete this book and has had faith in me for many years. His faith has inspired me to believe in myself.

To Jordan and Mack, you have been an energizing force in my life. Because of you, I started on this journey of learning all that I could in order to prepare you for the adult world. Thank you for being so patient and for growing into such amazing adults. You two are my legacy and my eternal bliss.

I am forever grateful for the guidance and direction of my editor, Jamie Santoro. Jamie has been a guiding light for me for many years and especially during the last year, which has been a difficult and trying time for so many of us. Jamie has motivated me and opened my eyes to new visions, and her pure positivity has definitely inspired me. Thank you, Jamie, for believing in me.

Last but not least, I want to thank my mentor Kathy Middleton, my amazing friends Sierra Campagna and Dunyau Maqsoudi-Moreno, and my CCCL colleagues. Thank you so much for all your support. To my dear readers, I am so grateful to have been able to work on such a captivating topic that is so relevant in today's world. I hope this book will invigorate and excite you to move forward and inspire our future generations of tomorrow.

Introduction

You've Got This!

I had a wonderful childhood, which is tough because it's hard to adjust to a miserable adulthood.　　　　　　　　　　　—LARRY DAVID

LET'S FACE IT, ADULTHOOD IS HARD. BETWEEN MAKING FINANCIAL DECISIONS, maintaining a healthy work–life balance, and juggling health, family, friends, and other responsibilities, life can sometimes feel overwhelming. Place these same responsibilities on an individual just entering adulthood who has less real-life experience and it can feel even more overwhelming. So why not make sure our teens and young adults are more prepared to face the world before they go out on their own? How can we also reinforce these skills for adults who may never have learned them or who may need a refresher?

We can do this by teaching life skills at the library. In this book, we break down what it means to be an adult and the required life skills needed to maintain a healthy, stable lifestyle. So what exactly are life skills?

Life skills refer to the basic skills that a person needs to navigate through life, such as financial management, career development, cooking, and self-care. At the library we can provide programs and activities that help patrons expand these life skills and accomplish their goals.

The Importance of Teaching Life Skills at the Library

When we offer life skills programs at the library, we can encourage our participants to imagine and prepare for real-world situations, such as planning a healthy meal, shopping for that meal, and cooking the meal at home. By doing this type of practice, we can help participants see how these skills are relevant to their lives and how they can practice them.

When teaching life skills programs, know that issues with social skills can come up. Remember that program participants, especially high school students, are still discovering who they are, and this can make every interaction in their lives feel monumental. If anyone attending is nervous, remind them that the library promotes a safe space and a relaxed environment. Participants should hopefully feel that when they attend a life skills class at your library. You can help create a relaxed environment by sharing a story about yourself when you were younger or by describing a skill that you didn't learn in school or from your parents, but rather had to figure out on your own. By sharing a relatable experience, you let the group know that they are not alone and that everyone struggles with learning new skills.

For many of us social skills are a given, but for others, it may not come as easily. I remember I was painfully shy in high school. I couldn't get up in front of class and speak; I had a hard time being in large groups. It took me many years to overcome my shyness. Those days are long gone now since I became a mom and a librarian. I have stretched my social skills far beyond those school days. These programs can help with building strong communication skills, as many activities focus on teamwork and working in small groups, where good communication is key. A great way to help your library community build these types of skills is by offering programs focused on life skills. In this book, we'll provide ideas for easy-to-implement activities that will keep attendees engaged and teach important life skills—everything from communication to budgeting. With all this information in your pocket, you will be able to put together your own life skills program with ease. Let's get started!

PART I

Planning Life Skills Programs

1

Let's Start Planning

Do you want to continue being great at being in your twenties, or do you want to step up and graduate into adulthood? —JASON BATEMAN

LIBRARY PROGRAM PLANNING HAS BECOME AN INCREASINGLY IMPORTANT aspect of our work. As we consider the needs of our community and decide which programs are most relevant, enriching, and engaging, we also need to keep in mind the importance of taking a strategic approach to program planning.

Establishing priorities, making decisions, and working within budget parameters are all part of the planning process. Collaborating with coworkers or community partners is an option that can greatly contribute to a program's success.

Where to Begin?

When I started working on the curriculum for my first life skills program, I thought about what might be the most important skills that someone would need to have when they were preparing to step out into the adult world. I could remember my own experiences clearly, and I can only imagine how it feels for someone who hears the words "living on your own" for the first time. After teaching life skills programs for several years now, I have noticed that there are many crucial skills that are necessary to know for living on your own. If you think about what a person needs to live on their own, you can see that the requisite knowledge and skills mostly involve what is needed to successfully manage living alone. Life skills are the tools that give a person the opportunity to learn and grow and fully experience each transition as it comes, which is the most meaningful way for a person to learn.

Creating interactive library classes and programs has always been one of the library's best hidden talents. So, let's get started with planning.

Goals and Objectives

If you want your life skills program to succeed, you need to set goals. Setting goals and objectives for the program will make the planning much easier and will allow you to take control of the direction that the program takes. When you set goals for your life skills program, you are also providing benchmarks for determining if the program was a success.

Goals can provide guidance on where you want to go with your program. A goal can be as simple as stating that the participants of the program will learn something new. You may even want to link your goals to your library's strategic plan. On the other hand, an objective is considered to be a more concrete step in the process that leads you to the completion of a goal. Objectives can also generate excitement and commitment, and can inspire program participants. The most satisfying part is being able to create a plan of action and chart a path to achieve your goals for the program.

Examples of goals include:

- Participants will sign up for programs in advance.
- Participants will receive handouts and class materials.
- Participants will explore life skills topics with hands-on activities.
- At least one presenter will be secured.

Hosts or Presenters

As you plan your program, you may be wondering whether you want to conduct it yourself or whether you want to invite a guest presenter. When I was planning my life skills programs, I really wanted to teach the participants myself instead of having an outside presenter come in. However, sometimes this doesn't always work if there is a topic that you are not super comfortable with.

For example, if you're planning a money management or financial planning program, you might want to have an expert from a financial organization do a presentation on all the intricate financial information needed. So you might want to think about this and decide what kind of environment you want to provide for your participants; if you want an engaging or inspiring program, you might want to present or host it yourself, or find a colleague you trust to collaborate with you. There are many ways to present life skills topics in an engaging way with slideshows and hands-on activities.

Topics

One of the most important factors in your life skills program will be what topics you will cover. You are free to decide what you'd like to cover in your program. For example, if you're doing a workshop on cooking, you might want to talk about the basics of food and nutrition and give an overview of how important grocery shopping and budgeting are. There are a lot of excellent YouTube videos that cover all kinds of topics that could be used for your workshop.

CHOOSING TOPICS

Things to consider:

- Think back to what you wish you had learned when you were younger.
- Look at what other libraries have done for their life skills programs.
- Present on a topic you are very knowledgeable about.
- Hire a presenter.

THE BIG THREE

There are many life skills that everyone needs to know, but the top three that I have found to be the most critical for these programs are Jobs/Careers, Money Management, and Cooking—whether it is conventional cooking or maybe an out-of-the-box, inventive style of cooking. Libraries can provide life skills programs to help patrons understand how to move through these unfamiliar topics and in turn approach a new phase in their lives. Libraries can thus help patrons to acquire new skills, bloom, succeed, and flourish.

Program Design

With all of the work that goes into cultivating a life skills program, it would be unfortunate if the participants did not retain what they learned. Developing a design style that includes hands-on activities can dramatically increase the participants' retention rates.

It's true, different people have different ways of learning, and the "one size fits all" philosophy is not always the best way to go when presenting a life skills program at the library. But with hands-on learning and activities, you will be able to keep most of the class intrigued and engaged at the same time, and that is a cause for celebration.

It's true that participants can sometimes space out even during the most engaging presentation. Sadly, this leads to missed opportunities for understanding and learning. But hands-on activities can keep your attendees interested, and when you think about it, it is hard for anyone to zone out while doing something fun and engaging. Moreover, if they know they will need to reproduce what they are being shown, they will be fully committed and much more attentive.

Ideas for Hands-on Activities

- Cooking in class
- Play a game
- Create a household budget
- Conduct mock interviews
- Practice résumé writing

Let's Plan a Life Skills Program: An Introduction to the Template

I hope you are excited about the possibilities and are ready to start making plans for a life skills program at your library. If we start with the Big Three, our focus will be on Finding a Job, Money Management, and Cooking Skills. One of the most important aspects of planning your life skills program will be to come up with a description of the program. You'll want to make sure that you have an interesting and catchy description that highlights what will be featured in the program.

Here is a life skills planning template for any one of the Big Three topics, and this template can be used as a guide as you plan your life skills program. The template has several sections:

- Program Title
- Program Description
- Goals and Objectives
- Topics Covered
- Activities

- Presenters
- Partners
- Marketing
- Evaluation

LIFE SKILLS PROGRAM PLANNING TEMPLATE

Your library's name

Program Title

Come up with a catchy title for your class—one that makes it clear what the topic is but which also appeals to your target audience. For example:

> Title: Ironed Chef Cooking
> Topic: Cooking: Food shopping, recipes, alternatives to traditional cooking

Program Description

Write a thorough description of the program. Include the date, time, length, and topics that will be covered. The following is an example:

We all need to nourish our bodies, and knowing how to cook is the best thing you can do for your own well-being. Who doesn't enjoy a delicious breakfast, lunch, or dinner? There's nothing more enjoyable than making your favorite food when you're hungry! Join us for our Ironed Chef cooking class next month, where we will be checking out our super cooking/ironing skills in real time.

> When: Thursday, October 21, 2022
> Where: World Cup Room
> For: Anyone who wants to learn how to cook
> Free event for all participants

(continued)

Goals and Objectives

What will participants be able to do as a result of participating in the class? What knowledge, skills, awareness, or abilities will they learn?

- Learn about grocery shopping skills.
- Read and understand nutrition labels.
- Practice simple cooking skills.

Topics Covered

What knowledge or skills will be introduced in the session?

- How to grocery shop
- Budgeting for groceries
- How to plan healthy meals
- Learn the concept of meal prepping
- Basic cooking skills
- Alternatives to conventional cooking

Activities

How will you make the session hands-on and interactive? What activities will help participants practice and apply the learning?

- Create a shopping list.
- Guess the price of a grocery item.
- Grocery scavenger hunt.
- Practice hands-on cooking skills.
- Use a clothes iron to make a delicious hot meal.

Presenters

Who will present the class? Include the person's name, title, and contact information:

Our Adult Services Librarian will be offering hands-on instruction on how to cook with a clothes iron.

Partners

Who are your partners for the class? And what role will they play? Will they provide resources (brochures, etc.)? Will they attend the session? Will they help market the session?

The Ironed Chef cooking class will be sponsored by the Friends of the Library, and we are excited to share a new partnership with local chef Juanita Gomez, the up-and-coming chef at the Serenity Vegan Restaurant.

Marketing

How will you get the word out about the class? What, when, and where will you promote the program in order to reach your target audience?

The Library will promote the Ironed Chef class by distributing flyers throughout the town and at the Serenity Vegan Restaurant. Flyers will also be distributed at local high schools and the community college campus.

Evaluation

How will you measure the success of the class? Will you create a survey for participants to take after the session? If so, what questions will you include?

An evaluation survey with questions regarding the class's effectiveness will be given to participants at the end of the program. Questions to be asked are:

- Did you enjoy this class?
- Do you feel that you learned the basics of grocery shopping?
- Did you learn any cooking skills?
- Are there other life skills programs that you would like to attend or recommend?
- Is there anything you would add to this class?

Partnership Opportunities and Program Promotions

I think becoming an adult and having to face up to your problems and face up to your insecurities is difficult for everybody.
— MARY ELIZABETH WINSTEAD, ACTRESS

PARTNERSHIPS CAN BE AN IMPORTANT PART OF YOUR LIBRARY ADULTING PRO-grams. Not all partnerships are perfect, but there is a lot of value in finding a partner for various reasons. We are looking for partners that will enhance the program, as well as add some support and hopefully some assistance with marketing and promotions. Sometimes it can be very helpful to partner with an organization or two if you are looking for new connections and opportunities to enhance your life skills program.

How to Find a Partner

There are many possibilities for partnership opportunities. The key is to do some networking and reach out to groups and organizations and ask if they would like to partner with the library. You might already know or work with someone that would be a great fit to partner with. Or, you might have someone else in mind who is a great cook or who works in a field that relates to the life skills topic you want to cover. The main challenge will be choosing the right partner, so look for those who share the same or similar goals and values, and the vision that you have for your program. Remember, there is always an opportunity to explore and expand. It may make sense to start with one solid partnership and grow from there.

Here are just a few ideas for partners that would be a good fit for a life skills program:

- Chamber of Commerce
- Nonprofit agencies
- Your city or county departments
- Local businesses
- Restaurants or bakeries
- Chefs or cooks
- Health services
- Colleges or schools
- Banks or credit unions
- Credit counselors

When thinking of partners, the sky is really the limit—as long as the partnership is a good fit for what you envision. Sometimes you'll find partners that can also provide a speaker for your program. You can help to offset the cost of your program by developing a program with a partner or sponsor that can contribute in-kind services, volunteers, and presenters.

Identifying Presenters

Looking for presenters can be a great way to reach out, connect with your community, and work with local organizations. In my experience, you can often find presenters who will present for free or for a small stipend, and who may be willing to share their knowledge with your program participants.

In lieu of finding a speaker or presenter, you may decide to plan and deliver a presentation yourself. When planning life skills programs at my library over the last several years, I have found that most of the time I prefer to conduct the programs myself or with a colleague. This is because I have a lot more control over how the program is presented, and I can make sure that the content and activities are fully relatable for the program participants. However, there are some types of programs that may need a presenter other than yourself, such as a program on financial literacy or on how to prepare your taxes. When you don't have the expertise yourself, that's an ideal time to look to your community to find a presenter.

One thing to consider is that you should always check out a speaker's presentation content in advance. You should at least ask to see an outline of the presentation before securing that person as a speaker. If it isn't exactly what you're looking for, you might ask if some changes can be made in it to suit your needs. Offer some feedback, and see if the presenter will make the changes. This will help to make the presentation the best fit for your audience. Here are some ideas on where to find presenters:

- Human Resources department (for someone to talk about hiring and job applications and interviews)
- Banks and credit unions (for money management)
- Restaurants, catering companies, or local school restaurant programs that offer cooking lessons or mobile chefs (cooking)
- Local hospitals, nurses, and cosmetologists (health and personal care)
- Therapist or mental health services (self-care)
- Toastmasters (public speaking)
- AARP or tax preparers (taxes)
- Colleagues with a special hobby (sewing, knitting, meditation, yoga, or gardening)

Marketing and Promotions

Marketing and promotions are very important to help get the word out about your upcoming life skills programs. Interesting promotional materials can let people know that there is a life skills program or workshop just for them.

In my experience in developing and implementing life skills programs at the library, I have found that one of the most important pieces of the puzzle is how they are promoted to the community. To succeed in recruiting an ample number of attendees, the promotions must be interesting and inviting. Since the library commonly has a reputation as a fairly chill place, we have the chance to reach out and promote this program as being in a safe space where everyone will be treated fairly. Another important fact to promote is that we are offering participants a chance to gain new skills in an environment that is non-judgmental.

When working on promotions for your life skills program, you'll want to consider your target age group. For a life skills program, this is most likely community members from ages 18 to 30, although it's possible you might have some attendees who are a bit older than that. You'll want to use all of the different types of media available to you when reaching out to the community. Remember, this is also a chance to highlight your library and the meaningful work that you are doing within the community.

Promotional plans can be both challenging and fun. Think about the various ways you can promote your program. Some ideas include:

- Create flyers and posters for your program.
- Promote the program on your library's website.
- Share on a variety of newsletters—those of the library, the Friends, and elsewhere in the city.
- Ask colleges or instructors to make announcements on campus.
- Post flyers on college campuses and in local businesses, cafes, bookstores, and restaurants.
- Create a social media campaign and post announcements and promotions on those outlets.
- Perform outreach at local colleges.
- Ask your partners and other libraries to spread the word.
- Make promotional buttons and have library staff wear them and give them out to the community.

Social media can be extremely helpful in promoting programs and workshops at the library. You can use as many platforms as you like, and all at one time if needed. My library uses Facebook and Instagram for our social media promotions. In addition to posting to your library's accounts, you should also make sure to follow local groups, schools, and clubs on all of those channels. They will probably follow you back, and that really helps when doing promotions. Here are some helpful tips when promoting a library adulting program on social media:

- Create a special hashtag just for your life skills programs and use it on all of your social media posts.
- Encourage sharing posts by creating engaging content and interesting headlines. The more people that share your posts the better.

- Consider livestreaming your program on Facebook. If you do this, your program will be completely live, and that can be very exciting! If you record the session, you can embed it on your library's website, and sharing your livestream is a great way to promote your future upcoming programs.
- Share updates on your upcoming life skills programs on Instagram. That is also a great place to share photos from your past programs (with permission, of course).
- Create a Facebook event for your life skills programs. Facebook events are perfect because you can invite anyone who has liked your library's page to your event. You can also make the event public so anyone can see it, and they can choose to attend. If they choose to attend, they should be reminded of the event before it happens.
- Promote special giveaways or perks that participants will receive if they attend the program.

Evaluate and Sustain Your Life Skills Programs

Be like the sun who falls in love with the moon and shares all his light.
—KAMAND KOJOURI

AFTER YOUR LIFE SKILLS PROGRAM HAS BEEN CONDUCTED, IT'S TIME TO evaluate your efforts. Evaluating how the program or workshop went is very important in order to understand what worked and what didn't work. In addition, you might want to think about sustaining your life skills program and keep it going by creating a unified series of such programs; a lot goes into creating a life skills program, and you'll see that it is really easy to duplicate the entire planning process. Your participants will enjoy these programs, so you may want to offer them on a regular basis.

Program Evaluation

There are several reasons why it's important to evaluate the programs that we offer. Evaluations can help us determine whether we've achieved the results or outcomes that we set at the beginning. Evaluation can help to identify any problems or areas that we need to improve upon, and it can also highlight what went well, too. This can help you improve the delivery of your next program. If you receive feedback on the program and how it went, you'll be able to gain ideas on how to better plan and promote for future programs.

EVALUATION QUESTIONS

These questions will help you create an effective evaluation plan:

- *What are you evaluating?* Your Life Skills program.
- *What criteria will be used to judge the class's performance?* The number of participants recruited for the program. The satisfaction of the participants. The feedback from participants through surveys, polls, or other data received. Was the program successful as a result of your efforts in planning and coordinating it?
- *What benchmarks should be met for the program to be considered successful?* You should create these benchmarks before the program starts and think about what you would consider for the program to be a success. For example, if at least 80 percent of the attendees stayed until the end of the program, or at least 80 percent of the attendees were satisfied with the program, then it was a success. You could also hope for at least 80 percent of the participants to give feedback on the program.

Sustaining Life Skills Programs

Sustaining your life skills program can be an easy thing to do because once you have gone through the entire process of creating one, you can save yourself a lot of time by simply duplicating the elements from program to program as you go. You can use the same life skills planning template, and you can take the same steps and create programs for the topics that you feel are the most relevant ones for your participants.

You may also be able to use the same marketing and promotional tools for each program, with only minor edits. In fact, you can often use the same materials and flyers, if you just change the topic and the description. By doing this you'll save time and even more importantly, you'll be creating a unified brand for your programs, with a consistent approach that will help the entire series flow together.

You can easily plan at least six months ahead just by using many of the important life skills topics covered in this book. If you are daring, you can plan a whole year of life skills programs in a series. A good time to start a life skills series is either in the fall or in the spring. I have tried to offer programs during the summer, and they are less well-attended because many people are away on vacation during that season.

Once you have embarked on the process of creating your first life skills program, creating a series will come easily and you can keep your programs going from month to month. Just think of all the benefits of a yearlong life skills series!

PART II

Life Skills Activity Plans

4

Jobs

If opportunity doesn't knock, build a door. —MILTON BERLE

LIFE SKILLS PROGRAMS ON THE DIFFERENT ASPECTS OF GETTING A JOB CAN provide opportunities for participants to identify the areas they excel in and the areas they need to develop. It's important to learn about the strengths and skills they already have and then apply these to different types of jobs in the work field. At the library, we can help participants learn how to apply for jobs with potential employers, as well as help them to learn how to set goals to find employment, which will help reduce any barriers they may be facing. Hands-on practice interviewing can also help them to prepare for obtaining a job.

Operation Job Application

Most employers expect job seekers to apply for jobs online. We can help our life skills participants search for jobs and create résumés, but they will also need to apply on the employer's website or on an online job board. Teaching participants how to navigate job-based websites can be as simple as going over computer skills, data processing, and teaching them how to upload a résumé and attach it to the application. With some hands-on practice, we can make this task much easier and more attainable.

LENGTH OF PROGRAM: 1–2 hours; Ask participants to sign up in advance.

MATERIALS OR RESOURCES NEEDED

- Computer lab if available
- Laptops (with a drive)
- Data stick (with résumé uploaded on it)
- Access to Wi-Fi
- Links for job-based websites
- Table and chairs
- Pens
- Paper

ACTIVITY

STEP 1. Give the students a short presentation covering the basics on how to browse for a file (their résumé) on the computer or drive and how to save their résumé as a PDF or Word document. The participants need to know the ins and outs of applying online, and this will give them a jump start.

STEP 2. Gather the participants in the computer lab or provide them with laptops and then let them practice applying for jobs online. They'll need their résumés for this activity, and having it on a data stick is a plus for uploading it on to online job applications. Guide the participants through the process of applying online, but first make sure that they have an e-mail account. You should also let them know that before they can apply for any job online, they will need to register with the job or company website. When applying, participants will get to experience the process of filling out the online application and adding all their information on to it. If they have their résumé on a data stick, they can practice uploading it to the job website as well.

ONLINE JOB APPLICATION SUPERPOWERS

Prepare your students to . . .

- Attach or upload a document.
- Keep a résumé on a data stick for easy uploading.
- Apply for multiple positions in order to cast a wider net.

Interview Prep Skills

The most important step in landing a job is being prepared for the interview. This is a life skill that many young people need to acquire. There are several points that we can teach our participants in order to prepare them for this crucial experience. One can never be too prepared, so activities that teach them to plan ahead is the key. This activity can give aspiring interviewees a leg up in the job interview process.

Length of Program: 1 hour

MATERIALS OR RESOURCES NEEDED
- Computer lab (if available)
- Laptops or tablets
- Access to Wi-Fi
- Table and chairs
- Pens
- Sheets of paper

ACTIVITY
This will be a fun activity that the whole class can join in on. It will help to convey the important elements needed for them to interview successfully, which include preparation, enthusiasm, eagerness, and a plan of action.

This activity allows the class to search online for potential employers' websites and find out as much as possible about the company before going to the interview. The class can use the list of employers that they applied for or companies that they found from their job search hunts.

STEP 1. Have the class sit at computers or use laptops and ask them to use a search engine of their choice to look for the companies on their lists. Once they find the company website, ask them to do a little detective work and check out the "About Us" page. This is a great way to find information on a company or other organization. Part of preparing for an interview is doing research on the place where you are interviewing because many employers ask questions like "What do you know about our company?" and "How do your skills fit with our company?" Job seekers should know what kind of company it is and what kinds of products it makes or services it provides. A good way to take a peek into the philosophy of the company is to check out its mission statement. A good question to ask the participants is: "Do you think you would fit in with this company, and if so, why?"

STEP 2. The second part of this activity is: if you have an interview, you need to find out where the location is before the appointment. This is another part of being prepared for the interview. Ask the class to find the address or location of a company on their list and then show them how to use Google Maps to find their interview destination in advance. This practice is really important and will help them to prepare to arrive at the interview on time, or early if possible.

INTERVIEW PREP SUPERPOWERS
Prepare your students to . . .

- Research potential employers and learn about their mission statements.
- Consider how they will get to an interview—driving, public transit, or ride.
- Find the location of their interview and plan to go to the interview on their own.

Mock Job Interviews

Practicing and planning for a job interview can be a very helpful tool. It is a great idea to include a life skills practicum that reviews the typical interview questions that will be asked at a job interview. Reviewing the possible answers can help participants come up with their own answers in advance. Helping them take the time to personalize their answers is a good way to show prospective employers that they are thoughtful and a good fit for the job.

LENGTH OF PROGRAM: 1–2 hours

MATERIALS OR RESOURCES NEEDED

- Practice interview questions
- Practice questions to ask the interviewers
- Sheets of paper
- Pens

ACTIVITY

Applying for a job for the first time can be a scary experience for anyone, especially if they don't have a lot of experience in the application and interviewing process. Practicing interviewing in advance can provide very positive benefits. The best strategy is to practice with mock interviews using role-playing, and to have participants practice answering questions, keeping eye contact, and using appropriate body language. This will help them to be genuinely prepared and will also boost their confidence. The motto for this activity is practice, practice, practice! The feedback from mock interviews can be enlightening and can give the participants a leg up in the interview process.

STEP 1. To get this activity started, ask the group if they have interviewed before, and what went well during their interview and what didn't go well. For great visuals, you can use a whiteboard: create two separate columns, and write in one column the positive comments and in the second column what the group found challenging. After this, hand out copies of the practice interview questions to the group. Ask them to review the questions and discuss as a group which ones they find to be the most difficult for them to answer. Next, review with the participants the practice questions to ask the interviewer. This is a great time to talk about what kinds of questions are appropriate to ask during an interview.

STEP 2. Let participants know that they should be prepared for the interview. The more information they have prepared in advance, the better impression they will make on the interviewer. They should take the time to print out a résumé and references if needed.

For some hands-on practice, ask the participants to pair up in groups of two and to take turns being the interviewer and the interviewee. This will give them a chance to hone their interviewing skills and learn new techniques. This is also a great way for them to get feedback from each other, and the practice will help them to be prepared when they go on a real interview. After the pairs have been both the interviewer and the interviewee, meet back up as a group to talk about how the mock interviews went. Ask them to share about their experience and how it felt to practice ahead of time. This activity will help them to prepare for a job interview and will also build confidence because knowing what to expect and being prepared are two very important aspects in the job hiring realm.

PRACTICE INTERVIEW QUESTIONS

- Why are you looking for a job?
- Why are you interested in working for us?
- How has school prepared you for working at a job?
- Are you able to work as a team member?
- Why should we hire you?

PRACTICE QUESTIONS TO ASK THE INTERVIEWERS

- What do the day-to-day responsibilities of the role look like?
- What's your favorite part about working at the company?
- What is a typical day at this company like?
- What are the next steps in the job process?

MOCK INTERVIEW SUPERPOWERS

Prepare your students to . . .

- Check out an interview simulation app like Hired or Go Interview for total preparation.
- Make eye contact with the interviewer, introduce themselves, smile, and be confident.
- Keep the communication positive, and relax.

Thank You for Your Time

We live in a digital world, but a handwritten note is still a very valuable tool in today's work world. One of the last steps in the job-hunting process is sending a thank-you note to the interviewer. This activity could help participants to make a big impact on a prospective employer. Handwritten notes are a fun way to say thank you. The life skills lesson here is that it only takes a few minutes to say thank you to someone for taking the time out of their day to meet you.

LENGTH OF PROGRAM: 1 hour

MATERIALS OR RESOURCES NEEDED

- Note cards (Thank you's or blank note cards will work)
- Pens (blue or black)
- Tables and chairs

ACTIVITY

STEP 1. Let the program participants know how important it is to follow up a job interview with a thank-you note. This can sometimes help prospective employers make a decision when they are hiring. Explain to the participants that although they can easily send an e-mail, it is a much nicer and more thoughtful touch to send a handwritten note in the mail.

STEP 2. Have the participants sit at the tables, and then pass out several note-cards for them to practice writing a thank you to an employer. Here are a few tips that you can give to participants:

- Open with a personal greeting and address the interviewer by name.
- Be sincere and authentic when expressing your gratitude or appreciation.
- Show that you care about the time the interviewer spent with you describing the details of the position.
- Restate that you are interested in the job.
- Refer to something you discussed in the interview.
- Identify what's particularly interesting to you about the position and explain why. This way, the note will feel more personalized.
- Refer to your skills and experience and show how you're going to use them to help your future employer get what they want.
- Always send a personalized thank-you note one day after the interview.

STEP 3. Make sure to cover how to close out or end the thank-you note. Here are a few more tips:

- Thank the interviewer again.
- Sign off with "sincerely" and write the interviewer's first and last name.
- Include basic contact details like your telephone number or e-mail address.

PRACTICE SAMPLE THANK-YOU NOTE

Hello [Interviewer's Name],

Thank you so much for taking the time to meet with me and talk about the position of the [Position Name] yesterday. It was a pleasure to learn more about your business approach.

Our conversation made me even more excited to join the [Company Name]. What interested me in particular was [something specific you discussed during the interview].

I'm sure my experience will be a great fit and I will be successful as your new [the name of the position you're applying for].

If you need any additional information from me at this point, please feel free to contact me. I'm looking forward to hearing back from you on [the specific date established during the interview]. Thanks again for your time!

Sincerely,

[Your Name]

NOTE-WRITING SUPERPOWERS

Prepare your students to . . .

- Send a personalized thank-you note one day after the interview.
- Write a thank-you note that demonstrates your strong interest in the job.
- Understand that many job candidates don't even send thank-you notes.

5

Money

*To acquire money requires valor, to keep money requires prudence,
and to spend money well is an art.* —BERTHOLD AUERBACH

MANAGING MONEY WISELY CAN SOMETIMES BE COMPLICATED, AND FOR SOME
it can be downright overwhelming. Budgeting and managing money and keeping a close eye on one's finances is a lifelong endeavor that everyone needs to learn. When preparing life skills participants for their future life, it really is important to go over something as important as money management. A life skills program with a focus on money management or financial literacy can help to give them a smooth transition into managing their own money and making the best financial decisions.

Show Me the Money

Money management is very important because things come up and banks charge fees for almost everything. It's important to clearly perceive the importance of money management and how bank accounts work. This activity is all about receiving money and then having it taken away. This game is definitely a learning experience, and when it comes to money, even when using pretend dollar bills, it can get very competitive and somewhat heated. There are definitely some high stakes in this game, but the goal is to teach the participants how important it is to focus on money management skills.

LENGTH OF PROGRAM: 1 hour

MATERIALS OR RESOURCES NEEDED

- Board game money
- Plain envelopes
- Markers
- Small pieces of paper
- Pens

ACTIVITY

STEP 1. You can use board game money for this one. Take a count of all your participants, and then place different amounts of money in envelopes and write a number on each envelope, so if you have ten participants you should have ten envelopes numbered one through ten.

STEP 2. Next, make little notes of paper or tickets with the envelopes' corresponding numbers on them and place the tickets in a hat. Hand each person an envelope with a number on it. Then have each person draw a ticket. If they draw the number out of the hat with the same number on the envelope that they hold, they are safe. If not, they must find the person who holds the envelope with their number on it. They must make an appeal to this person and ask them if they can keep their money instead of giving it up to them. It's up to the person holding the money to decide if they want to give it back or not. This is a fun activity that shows participants what it's like to have money and then if something suddenly comes up, they lose the money.

MONEY SUPERPOWERS

Prepare your students to . . .

- Imagine money is a person in their life and treat it well.
- Build an emergency money fund.
- Focus on long-term, money-saving goals.
- Study all they can about money management and learn to hold on to their money.

Needs vs. Wants Tournament

Understanding needs vs. wants is very important for money management and budget planning. Needs are important because they represent the necessities, while wants can improve the quality of a person's life. In this activity, the focus will be on determining what the necessities in life are and how to fit the rest—the wants—into a budget. The goal for this activity is to work out a budgeting plan and learn how to manage money carefully.

LENGTH OF PROGRAM: 1 hour

MATERIALS OR RESOURCES NEEDED

- Recycled card decks (4 or 5 of them)
- Printout photos of things that are either needs or wants
- Glue

ACTIVITY

STEP 1. Create the needs/wants card decks in advance by recycling old decks of playing cards (52 cards in a deck). You'll want to have one deck for needs and one deck for wants. Make a list of needs and wants. For example, vacations and concerts would fall under wants, whereas shoes and groceries would fall under needs. Recycle magazines or search online and print out the images of needs and wants in color, and then cut out and glue the photos on the recycled cards. You might want to get some helpers for this.

STEP 2. For this session, start out with a brief overview of needs vs. wants. Explain that needs are the things that are essential for us to be able to live. They are the recurring expenses that are likely to eat up a large chunk of our money. Wants are expenses that help you live more comfortably or enjoyably. They're the things you buy for fun or because you just gotta have it. You could live without them, but life would be so much more enjoyable if you were able to get these things. For instance, food is a need, but daily lunches at an expensive restaurant fall into the wants category. After the needs vs. wants overview, divide the class into groups of 4 or 5 participants. Give each group a deck of cards.

STEP 3. Explain to them that they are going on a journey to explore life in another galaxy. Their task is to choose what they will bring with them. Then surprise them with the most important part of the activity. They can't take everything they want! They can only take 10 items, and each group's members must collectively decide what to bring, out of the 52 choices on each deck of cards. This puts the pressure on, and they will have to decide what they absolutely need and then decide what "wants" they can live without. This should be a very engaging activity, with a lot of discussion and collaborating within each group.

NEEDS VS. WANTS SUPERPOWERS

Prepare your students to . . .

- Make tough decisions about what they need as opposed to what they want.
- Save money for a rainy day so they can treat themselves to something they really want.
- Decide if they can live without something they want.

Financial Literacy Jeopardy

Financial literacy is the ability to make informed judgments and effective decisions about the use and management of money. Financial literacy is critical because it provides us with the knowledge and skills we need to manage our money effectively. Understanding financial topics and how we can manage our money can make an impact on almost every aspect of our lives.

Length of Program: 1.5 hours

MATERIALS OR RESOURCES NEEDED

ACTIVITY

- Laptop
- Projector and screen
- Wi-Fi
- JeopardyLabs website (https://jeopardylabs.com/play/financial-literacy-jeopardy)
- Tables and chairs
- Paper
- Pencils

Here's a great way for the entire class to learn about financial literacy and also play a fun game.

STEP 1. You'll want to set the tables up in the room so that all of them face the projector screen. If participants aren't familiar with how the game of Jeopardy is played, go over the specifics and let them know that they have to give their answer in the form of a question, for example, "What is a savings account?"

STEP 2. The website JeopardyLabs has an interactive game already set up, and all you need to do is get your laptop, projector, and screen set up and pull up this amazing site. Who doesn't love a fun game of Jeopardy? This is a great way to cover everything about money and financial expenses with your life skills program, right down to learning about emergency and sinking funds. Emergency funds are somewhat self-explanatory, but sinking funds are planned for bigger items and are expenses that don't happen very often, like taxes or gift-giving for the holidays. Learning about financial literacy can be fun and can spark interest with an interactive game of Jeopardy.

FINANCIAL LITERACY SUPERPOWERS
Prepare your students to . . .

- Pay special attention to their money.
- Keep their money secure in a bank account.
- Be conservative with their money and make good financial decisions.

Travel Time

Traveling can be a great thing to do if you save money for it and plan ahead. Teaching a life skills program the importance of planning ahead for a trip is really essential. There are so many factors to be covered in this activity. Life skills is about teaching participants how to do and try new things, so trips and vacations fall right into that realm. This activity will help acquaint them with the trip-planning process by learning to budget how much money they can spend on a trip.

LENGTH OF PROGRAM: 1 hour

MATERIALS OR RESOURCES NEEDED

- Premade list of questions
- Map of the United States
- Colored push pins
- Computer lab or classroom
- Laptops or tablets
- Wi-Fi
- Tables and chairs
- Paper
- Pencils

ACTIVITY

The purpose of this activity is for the participants to plan financially for a trip. It can be any kind of trip, one for fun or one for discovery and exploration. It can help if the participants look for discount airfares or check the prices on traveling by bus or train. As for lodging, they can look at Airbnb's, hotels, or else plan to stay with a relative. The key is to find a way to go on a fantastic trip and spend as little as possible.

PART 1. Hang the map of the United States up on the wall where everyone can reach it. Also, have ready a travel worksheet with the questions that are listed below. Ask the group to look at the map and decide where they want to go. Then ask them to answer the following questions on the worksheet:

- Where is your destination?
- What is your travel budget? Example: $2,000
- Where will you stay? Example: hotel, Airbnb, relative
- How long will your trip last? Example: 2 weeks
- When will you travel? Example: June 1–14

PART 2. Ask everyone to go to the map on the wall. Once everyone has completed their worksheet, ask each of them to put a colored push pin on the destination that they chose.

PART 3. Next, ask participants to use their travel worksheets to do some research on their laptop or computer. Give them a list of travel planning sites to use and help them to look up how much it will cost to fly to their destination and back home. Some sites are really easy to navigate, like StudentUniverse .com, where you can search for everything you need such as air flights, hotels, and car rentals, all in one place. This activity is more about planning for a trip than about saving up money for one. It will give participants an idea of how much it really costs to go on a vacation and how much money they will need to save to get to their chosen destination.

TRAVEL PLANNING SUPERPOWERS

Prepare your students to . . .

- Create a special savings fund for vacation money.
- Cut back on their expenses to save a little more for travel time.
- Make a vacation spending plan and stick to it.

6

Cooking

Always start out with a larger pot than what you think you need.

—JULIA CHILD

LEARNING HOW TO COOK AND FINDING TIME TO COOK ARE VERY IMPORTANT skills that everyone should have. Life skills programs can help participants to learn to cook for themselves, try out new recipes, and enjoy eating healthier foods. We can also teach them about healthy eating options that involve cooking meals at home, instead of eating fast food and junk food. Making a shopping list and preparing meals ahead of time are just a few ways that this can be done. Program participants will discover how easy it is to find recipes and cook meals with just a little practice.

Shopper's Delight

Grocery shopping is a very important life skill to have. It plays an important role in the realm of cooking, and students can control what they buy (and consume) by sticking to the items on their shopping list. Shopping for food can also be a very calming experience. Strolling through the aisles, perusing what's on the shelves, and looking at all the colorful fruits and vegetables in the produce section can play a positive role in learning how to cook. Grocery shopping can be more fun if you plan ahead and create a shopping list, and this activity will be the perfect way to practice.

LENGTH OF PROGRAM: 1 hour

MATERIALS OR RESOURCES NEEDED

- 8½ × 11 sheets of white paper
- Clip art to create "aisles" for produce, dairy, meat, bakery, dry goods, and frozen foods
- Glue to attach the clip art to paper
- Scratch paper
- Pens
- Pencils
- Grocery store coupons
- Various fruits for prizes

ACTIVITY

STEP 1. Here's something fun to do to get started and plan ahead for this activity. You should bone up on how to create a grocery shopping list on a budget, or on how to shop in a healthy and affordable way. Check out some of the grocery shopping blogs on sites like Eat This, Not That! (www.eatthis.com) and Z.E.N. Foods (https://zenfoods.com). They offer excellent advice on grocery shopping.

STEP 2. You will need to make some visuals ahead of time that will help participants do their own grocery shopping. Make the shopping aisles by gluing clip art on to white paper to make faux shopping aisles. You should end up with six aisles standing for produce, dairy, meat, bakery, dry goods, and frozen foods. You can put the shopping aisle sheets in a plastic protector to make sure that they don't get torn.

STEP 3. For the shopping list, any kind of paper can be used to make a list, so make sure everyone has plenty of paper. You can also pass out the store coupons to each participant and ask all the participants to take a look at the shopping aisles you have created. Give them around three to five minutes to peruse the coupons in order to get an idea of what kinds of food they might want to buy.

STEP 4. Ask the students to make a grocery list covering the various faux food aisles and let them know that if they can match coupons to the items they choose, they will get a discount off their total. Then see who gets the most discounts from their grocery coupons. The winner should get a prize from an item on their list, like apples or bananas.

GROCERY SHOPPING SUPERPOWERS

Prepare your students to . . .

- Create a list of grocery items that helps to prioritize their spending and save time and energy.
- Cross items off their shopping list once they put them in their cart.
- Look for items on sale and use coupons to buy them.
- Buy the items that are on their list and stay on budget

A Week of Dinners

Preparing ahead of time to make dinner is something we can all learn to do. Teaching participants about the importance of meal planning will get them ready for when they are living on their own. Showing the participants how to think ahead can also help them to maintain nutritionally well-balanced dinners throughout the week. For example, planning ahead can ensure that dinners have all the right veggies, protein, and grains, and helps to satisfy individual nutrition needs.

LENGTH OF PROGRAM: 1 hour

MATERIALS OR RESOURCES NEEDED

- A variety of cookbooks (look for book donations)
- Paper
- Pens and pencils
- Ideas for healthy dinners
- Tables and chairs

ACTIVITY

This activity is a great way for participants to learn how to plan ahead for meals, and also to learn how to read a cookbook.

STEP 1. Gather together as many cookbooks as you can and put them all on a table for display. Have participants look through the cookbooks and choose seven dinner recipes, one for each day of the week. After they have chosen the recipes, ask them to write out a grocery shopping list containing all the items they will need to cook the meals they chose. You could also ask them to think about tailoring the dinners to meet dietary issues like cooking for vegetarians or vegans.

STEP 2. Once the students have completed their shopping lists, ask the group to share some of the meals they chose. Another fun thing to do would be to ask them to explain why they chose the meals they did, and ask them if they want to take their lists home and try the recipes out.

MEAL PLANNING SUPERPOWERS

Prepare your students to . . .

- Save time, reduce stress, and eat healthier by meal prepping (i.e., preparing whole meals or large dishes in advance that will last for several days).
- Be more confident in the kitchen.
- Know what ingredients are in the food they're eating.

Smoothie Stations

We all know that eating healthy can sometimes be difficult. Busy schedules, tight budgets, and the difficulty of cooking are all challenges that hinder us from making good nutritional choices. However, it is possible to create a healthy and balanced meal just by putting together special ingredients to make a smoothie. Your life skills program is going to love this healthy and delicious activity.

LENGTH OF PROGRAM: 1 hour

MATERIALS OR RESOURCES NEEDED

- Several electric blenders (one for each smoothie recipe)
- Printout of several smoothie recipes
- Smoothie ingredients, such as bananas, oranges, strawberries, or blueberries, along with milk or almond milk, and protein powder
- Cups
- Ice chest
- Ice
- Tables for smoothie stations

ACTIVITY

This is a really rewarding and tasty activity to do with a group. All you need are several blenders and supplies for smoothie ingredients. These can be assorted fruits such as bananas, strawberries, and blueberries. You can make dairy or nondairy smoothies, and ice is usually a great addition to make them nice and cold.

STEP 1. Before the program starts, set up several smoothie stations, which are tables with a blender, ice, cups, and smoothie ingredients. Let the group know that it's up to them to find the smoothie station of their choice. The trick for this activity is to have each participant make their own smoothie and design it to their own taste. So, once they choose their favorite smoothie station, they will get a chance to put all the ingredients together and blend, blend, blend.

STEP 2. After all the smoothies are complete, ask the group to make a toast to their smoothie-making success. Cheers!

HEALTHY SMOOTHIE SUPERPOWERS

Prepare your students to . . .

- Eat a healthy smoothie for breakfast and get the key nutrients they need.
- Boost their fruit and vegetable intake.
- Add protein and fiber to a smoothie for fuel and energy.

Pizza Perfection

Cooking is a valuable life skill that encompasses both nutrition and preserving the quality of food. Pizza is an incredible meal that many people love. Life skills are all about learning new things, and what better way is there to learn to cook than by making pizza? Some special things covered in this activity are: where does pizza come from, and how is it made? This activity covers many things that will help participants with cooking and nutritional values. Help your program participants become excited about cooking by exploring simple and easy ways to create the wonderful food we call pizza.

LENGTH OF PROGRAM: 2 hours (1 hour for each activity)

MATERIALS OR RESOURCES NEEDED

- Laptop
- Projector
- Projector screen
- Paper plates
- Pizza cutter
- Several bags of pita bread
- Pizza sauce (out of a jar, or make your own)
- Several bags of grated mozzarella cheese
- A variety of pizza toppings—pepperoni, salami, sliced mushrooms, black olives, sliced onions, and anything else you want to add
- Toaster oven
- Tables and chairs
- Paper
- Pens or pencils
- Fun facts about pizza

ACTIVITY

This activity is all about pizza, so you really can't go wrong here.

STEP 1. The best way to start out is to have a slideshow prepared so you can talk about various aspects of pizza. You will first want to cover where pizza originated. Pizza has been around since the eighteenth century and originated in Naples. There are also many different styles of pizza, such as New York, Chicago, California, and Neapolitan. Each of these has a unique type of crust and ingredients. Let participants know what the main ingredients of a pizza are. These are usually the main ingredients: crust, sauce, cheese, and toppings such as meat, veggies, or sometimes even fruit.

Next, give a brief overview of the main food groups. Let them know about grains (breads, cereals, rice, pasta, noodles), dairy (milk and cheese), fruits, vegetables, and protein (meat, eggs, and nuts). After you have covered the main food groups, you can ask the participants to decide what food groups are in a pizza. For example, the crust falls into the category of grains. The cheese is in the dairy group, and the red sauce falls into either the fruit or vegetable group (as tomatoes are considered to be both). The toppings are usually meat and vegetables. It would be great to have pictures of these items up on the screen while you're going through each of the food groups.

Another fun addition to the activity would be to quiz the participants on which ingredients in pizza provide the most nutrition. A great way to do this would be to make flash cards with each ingredient on a card. Write the nutritional value of each ingredient on the back of the card so the participants can't see it. Ask them to guess how many calories are in the different pizza ingredients. The person who gets the closest number gets to make their pizza first!

STEP 2. Make a perfect pita pizza in program. To do this part of the activity you will need the pizza essentials:

- Pita bread, pizza sauce, cheese, and all the toppings
- Paper plates and a pizza cutter

Ask everyone to grab a pita, some cheese, and their favorite topping and put it all on a paper plate. Hand out tiny bowls for the sauce. Make sure to have several spoons on hand. Here is the fun part: it is time to start layering the items on the pita bread. The best way to layer a pizza is to put the sauce, then the cheese, and then the toppings on the pita bread (or pizza dough, for that matter). Once you've talked about the layering, let everyone make their own personal pizza. All they need to do is put a pita on a paper plate and then layer it any way they want. Let them know that they can add as many or as few toppings as they choose. After the perfect layering has been completed, it's time to put the pizza into the toaster oven.

STEP 3. To start this part, shift the conversation a little and ask the program participants if they know how a pizza is cooked. There are a couple of ways that pizzas are traditionally cooked, either in an oven or a fire pit. For this activity, you are going to use a toaster oven. It works really well, and the outcome will be a delicious personal-sized pizza. How long do you cook a pizza in a toaster oven? If you only have one toaster oven, you may want to stagger the pizza-layering shifts so the wait for cooking is not too long. Once in the oven, it should only take about five minutes to heat up and to melt the cheese. Be careful, the pizza will be a bit hot, so let it cool off for a minute or two. It's also fun to use the pizza cutter to create those famous triangular slices we love so much. While the group is eating their perfect little pizzas, you can share fun facts about pizza and ask them if they know that celebrities love pizza too. It's a well-known fact that many stars love pizza, and it's unanimously agreed that pizza fixes everything.

PIZZA PREP SUPERPOWERS

Prepare your students to . . .

- Learn about nutritional values.
- Find their favorite toppings.
- Make a healthy and delicious pizza.

7

Self-Care

Be patient with yourself. Self-growth is tender; it's holy ground. There's no greater investment.
— STEPHEN COVEY

IN TODAY'S WORLD, IT'S HARD TO FIND A MOMENT'S PEACE. BETWEEN WORK or school, home life, and the many other projects in life, there's little time left in the day to reflect. Teaching participants about self-care is very important because we need to give them the tools they need to learn how to relax and de-stress. It's important for students to practice self-care so they can maintain healthy boundaries for themselves. Though it's not easy to do, it's important for them to find time to unplug and focus on their well-being. The activities in this chapter focus on teaching self-care practices and encouraging participants to find time for themselves.

The Twelve Cards of Self-Care

Self-care is more than just taking care of ourselves. It's about taking time to stop doing busy work and spend time focusing more introspectively. There are many ways that we can teach and promote good self-care. We can help our life skills participants focus on relaxation, inner peace, and self-improvement. We can also teach them that practicing self-care is about taking breaks or stepping away from anything stressful. It takes time to learn how to practice self-care, and this activity is all about learning different ways to practice.

LENGTH OF PROGRAM: 1 hour

MATERIALS OR RESOURCES NEEDED

- Card stock paper (enough to make 24 cards)
- Clip art of self-care aspects (examples given below)

ACTIVITY

This activity helps participants to recognize the various components of good self-care and to identify positive ways to improve their self-care.

STEP 1. To start off, explain to the group that self-care encompasses many different aspects. These include rest and relaxation and other healthy and healing habits. Let them know that one of the best things to do for self-care is to start a routine or habit of doing things that are good for their well-being. Some examples that you can use for the clip art on the twelve cards are things like going on a walk, fishing, creating art, yoga or meditation, and eating healthy foods. Some people even think that shopping is a great form of self-care. The key in self-care is to clear and de-stress the mind, and try something new or make self-improvements of some kind. You can also brainstorm with the class some ideas that they have and what self-care means to them.

STEP 2. To start the game, only twelve can play at a time. Each person in the group gets a card that will have an aspect or representation of self-care on it. Each person will have a chance to talk about their card and what it means to them. They will also need to answer these questions about their card:

- Is this picture showing good self-care?
- Give an example of self-care that you are already doing.
- Give an example of self-care that you are not doing that you would like to do.

After each person gets a chance to talk about their card, open up the floor for questions. This is a great time for a discussion on self-care. Also, make sure to let everyone know that they are in a safe space and what they share will not go outside of the group. To wrap things up, remind everyone that they have shared some great ideas about self-care and ask them to think about something they can easily do to improve their self-care.

SELF-CARE SUPERPOWERS

Prepare your students to . . .

- Find a routine for self-care and stick to it.
- Intentionally plan self-care activities, instead of just hoping that something happens.
- Keep a keen eye on what works, and cultivate those helpful self-care practices.

Creativity Is Calling

Having a creative outlet is something that we can all take to heart. Spending time on something creative is a time to express our thoughts and feelings. It is also very important for self-preservation and well-being. Life skills participants should be encouraged to explore different outlets to boost their self-expression and creativity. Your program could be about journaling, writing poetry, painting, drawing, photography, dancing, or any other creative outlet. The key here is to have your group channel their emotions through whatever medium they choose. This activity is about investigating different avenues of creativity, clearing their minds, and feeling the happiness of creating something unique.

LENGTH OF PROGRAM: 1 hour

MATERIALS OR RESOURCES NEEDED

- As many art supplies as you can find
- Paint, watercolors, colored markers, ink pens
- Paper, fabric, ribbon, anything textured
- Notebooks and journals
- Glue, tape, and glue dots
- Tables and chairs
- Plastic table covers

ACTIVITY

STEP 1. To start this fun and engaging activity, let the participants know that they don't have to worry about not being good at drawing or painting. The point of this activity is to not think about anything and just let their inner creativity come out. It's all about self-expression and finding an outlet in order to relax and de-stress. Let them know that they don't have to create something perfect. There are many ways to be creative, and working with mixed media and creating crafts are perfect for this activity. Creating crafts is also very relaxing because the mind is able to take a break and just go with the flow during the process. It's as if the mind becomes immersed in the process of creating something. A tip for getting started with this activity is to play some music that is engaging and fun in the background.

STEP 2. Let the group know that they can create their own journals, and then provide them with paper and notebooks and art supplies. Set up everything on a table and give them five to ten minutes to pick out the items they want to work with. Once they have all the supplies they need, it's time to let their creativity come out. The best thing of all is that working in a creative state can help to get rid of negative thoughts or feelings. Let them give way to their feelings during the activity, and then ask them if they think it was a good way to do self-care. At the end of the activity, ask the group how they felt when they were spending time in their own creative space. Most of them will agree that spending time making crafts, creating art, and even journal writing are all great ways to practice self-care.

CREATIVITY SUPERPOWERS
Prepare your students to . . .

- Be inspired by music.
- Spend time in nature.

All the Feels

Have you heard of Random Acts of Kindness or RAKs before? This is when someone does an unexpected act of charity or kindness for another person. Focusing on RAKs is a perfect activity for life skills participants because they can practice on anyone who needs to have a kind deed done for them. Examples might include paying for someone's coffee, helping a person across the street, or offering to say hello to a crying baby while the parents finish shopping. The great thing about this activity is that it can also be done for friends and family members. Your life skills program will agree that this activity is perfect for self-care.

LENGTH OF PROGRAM: 1 hour

MATERIALS OR RESOURCES NEEDED

- 100 blank note cards
- Assorted stickers
- Colored markers and pens
- Metallic markers
- Tables and chairs

ACTIVITY

Helping others can be a great way to bring about positivity and well-being. Some people find that their own problems seem less severe when they help others. While a Random Act of Kindness is definitely not a substitute for mental health treatment, it can help people feel better about themselves and those around them.

STEP 1. There are a number of ideas that center around showing kindness to someone unexpectedly. To begin with, let the participants know about Random Acts of Kindness and how it works. The whole concept was started in 1995 and because it became so popular, the Random Acts of Kindness Day is now on February 17. There is also a nice quote about RAKs by the actor Morgan Freeman: "How do we change the world? One random act of kindness at a time." This beautiful quote exemplifies the purpose of RAKs and helps to clarify what the term means.

STEP 2. This activity is a simple way to help participants show kindness and practice self-care, so it's a win-win project for everyone. Ask each member of the group to choose up to ten note cards and let them know that it's up to them to customize them. Give them the following list of short, positive blurbs as ideas for what they can put on their note cards.

- Have a beautiful day.
- Hey, you're awesome!
- Your smile is like sunshine.
- Keep up the great work!

Give the group time to work on their cards, and let them get as creative as they want. They can decorate the inside of the card and the envelope, too.

STEP 3: NOW FOR THE LAST PART. Tell the group that when they are done, they get to take the cards home with them and they can pass out the cards to anyone they like. They can give a card to someone who provides a service to them, like the barista at the coffee shop or their mail carrier. They can give one to a classmate who looks like they're having a bad day and needs some positive energy. The hope is that the participants will give away all ten of the cards that they decorated and in turn make ten people's lives a little better.

KINDNESS SUPERPOWERS

Prepare your students to . . .

- Plan small acts of kindness like giving a card to someone.
- Be kind and spread positivity.
- Understand how acts of kindness promote compassion and a sense of interconnectedness.

Who Let the Dogs In?

Many dogs are loyal and affectionate, thus making them the best companions around. Petting a dog can be a serious mood booster. Apparently, just gazing into a dog's eyes can make you feel good. Offering a life skills program where participants can spend time playing with dogs will offer them a variety of tools to manage stress. Touch and movement are two healthy ways to quickly manage stress, which is highly important for self-care. Petting a dog, cat, or other fuzzy animal can quickly help you feel calmer and less stressed. With this activity you'll be offering participants a chance to learn a few ways to de-stress. Plus, they'll be spending time with dogs, and that really can't be beat.

Length of Program: 1 hour

MATERIALS OR RESOURCES NEEDED

- Meeting room or quiet space
- Pillows or beanbag chairs
- Chairs
- Bowls for water
- Therapy dogs
- Books (preferably ones about dogs)

ACTIVITY

STEP 1. The best way to start this one is to plan ahead and have therapy dogs visit. You'll want to work with a local organization that promotes humane education and the adoption of rescue animals, and which offers dog teams to visit the library. Make sure to schedule several dog teams. A dog team consists of a dog handler and a dog who is trained as a registered therapy dog that can work with people of all ages and all abilities. Many of these dog teams are amazing because they are nonjudgmental and have a warm and fuzzy brand of understanding.

STEP 2. For the main event, you'll want to set up the room with comfy chairs, beanbag chairs, or pillows on the floor. Make sure to have some regular chairs for those who don't want to sit on the floor. Before the dogs arrive, let the group know that part of self-care is finding ways to relax and reduce stress, and one of the best ways to do this is to spend time with a companion animal. There are so many benefits to spending time with therapy dogs, and in this activity, participants can choose what they'd like to do. They can spend time with one dog team, or they can choose to visit with all of the dog teams. They can also find a book that they want to read to a dog. This is a relaxing way to spend time, and the dogs really love to be read to. (This activity can also help people become better readers.) Bringing together therapy dogs for a self-care life skills program will create a calm and serene atmosphere that the entire group can enjoy.

DOG PETTING SUPERPOWERS

Prepare your students to . . .

- Stay calm and approach dogs slowly.
- Learn how to pet a dog.
- Have their mood boosted.
- Know that dogs are excellent at interpreting our tone of voice, body language, and gestures.

Personal Care

We're a walking billboard.... You want to look good to everyone who is wataching.
                                                                —CHANDLER PARSONS

PERSONAL CARE IS A TOPIC THAT MAY SEEM A BIT SENSITIVE IN NATURE. HOW-
ever, this may be one of the most important life skills topics to cover because some people have difficulty with personal care. When teaching participants about personal care you can encompasses many aspects, such as bad breath, insufficient showering, or tangled hair, to name just a few. Personal care is also a significant factor in maintaining good health, as well as cultivating positive social interactions. Providing your life skills program with a few tools to tackle personal care can be done quite easily. There are some simple and fun solutions that can be covered in a library life skills program or workshop.

Personal Care Charades

The good news is that personal care can be improved through life skills programs at the library. Over time, practicing daily routines can be incorporated, and playing a fun game of charades can also help to improve our understanding of some of the most important concepts of personal care.

55

LENGTH OF PROGRAM: 1 hour

MATERIALS OR RESOURCES NEEDED

- Meeting room
- Tables and chairs
- List of personal care actions

ACTIVITY

Help everyone get the notions of personal care right by playing a game of good old-fashioned charades.

STEP 1. Have a list of personal care actions ready for the game. Write them all down on pieces of paper, and then fold these up and place them in a hat or basket.

STEP 2. Have each person in the group choose a piece of paper from the basket and read it to themselves. Make sure they know not to say the action out loud. Once they have read it, they will have to act out the action. For example, if they chose brushing your teeth, they would have to do the motions of how that looks when they brush their teeth. The only catch is that they have to do this without using any words. The group can call out what they think the action is, and each person gets a point if they can name the correct action. After each charade, it would be a good time to talk about the proper way to do each personal care and why it's important to practice a regular routine.

LIST OF PERSONAL HYGIENE ACTIONS

- Brushing teeth
- Taking a shower
- Washing hair
- Sanitizing hands
- Covering mouth when sneezing
- Clipping nails
- Flossing teeth
- Getting a good night's sleep
- Putting on deodorant
- Spraying on cologne or perfume

PERSONAL CARE SUPERPOWERS

Prepare your students to . . .

- Understand the importance of personal care.
- Have a daily personal care routine.
- Keep their skin and hair clean.
- Learn that good personal care is important for good health.

Washington's Teeth

Have you ever seen what George Washington's false teeth looked like? They're kind of wild and a bit scary. You can use Washington's teeth as a platform to teach your program about personal dental care. The teeth that we see in portraits of Washington were not made of wood as we once thought. Washington's dentures were made of human and animal teeth and elephant ivory. The dentures were held together with brass wires and steel springs. Focusing on Washington's teeth is a great way to kick off a program on the importance of dental care.

LENGTH OF PROGRAM: 1 hour

MATERIALS OR RESOURCES NEEDED

- Laptop
- Projector
- Projector screen
- Tables and chairs set up in classroom style

ACTIVITY

Our teeth play a very important role in our lives because they enable us to chew our food, which is crucial for digesting it properly. The consequences of poor dental care can be devastating and sometimes even painful. This activity gives a somewhat humorous outlook on what happens if you don't take care of your teeth. It's an interesting way to share an important life skill by taking a trip back in time to look at what George Washington's false teeth looked like in the late eighteenth century.

STEP 1. Start by showing participants pictures of Washington's dentures and give them some good ones to look at. The teeth are brown and yellow and really misshapen. Showing these photos will open up a great discussion on how brushing our teeth regularly relates to personal health and personal care.

STEP 2. Talk about why George Washington had false teeth and what they were made of. Show a few short videos that give this activity an interesting historical viewpoint. One video made directly by the Mount Vernon Preservation Society is called *Did George Washington Have Wooden Teeth?* The video is only about two minutes long, but it gives some interesting information about the history of Washington's teeth. Another video by Atlas Obscura called *Behold, George Washington's Last Tooth* offers a look at one of Washington's dentures and his last (real) tooth, which his dentist kept in a locket.

STEP 3. Wrap us the program by having a group discussion of what they learned from George Washington's teeth and the importance of good dental health.

TEETH CLEANING SUPERPOWERS
Prepare your students to . . .

- Brush and floss every day.
- Share a healthy and happy smile.
- Prevent tooth loss.

The Art of Packing a Suitcase

Packing a suitcase is an art form that many of us should try to master. Packing can be as difficult as putting together a puzzle. Teaching your life skills program how to manage the difficulty of fitting everything they need into a suitcase or travel bag will help them to understand the process. This activity will help students practice packing and will be a great way to teach participants how to organize every inch of their suitcase.

LENGTH OF PROGRAM: 1 hour

MATERIALS OR RESOURCES NEEDED

- Several suitcases
- Backpacks
- Different articles of clothing
- Shoes or sandals
- Socks and scarves
- Small pillows or stuffed animals
- Luggage tags or note cards for prizes

ACTIVITY

Here's your chance to get really creative and make packing for a trip into a game that you play with program participants. This activity involves folding or rolling clothing and other items, as well as planning and organizing skills.

STEP 1. Each person will need a suitcase, although a backpack would work very well for this activity too. Give them each a pile of clothing along with items like shoes, sandals, and even a pillow to make it more engaging.

STEP 2. Divide the group into teams of two. Each team member will get a turn at packing. The goal of the activity is to see if the teams can get all of their belongings packed and their suitcases closed or zipped up without having to sit on it. The winner should receive a prize like luggage tags or note cards for their ingenuity and resourcefulness.

PACKING SUPERPOWERS

Prepare your students to . . .

- Pack a suitcase.
- Roll clothes instead of folding them.
- Put small items like socks inside shoes.

Photo Booth Fun

It's true that some people may have difficulty understanding the importance of personal care. No worries, you can teach your life skills program exactly what they need to know. With this activity, you can also give them a reminder of how important personal care and grooming are in the adult world. Personal care is absolutely a necessity if they want to interact with others socially. That's why this activity is a great way to promote personal care and make it into an entertaining activity where everyone gets dazzled up for a festive photo shoot.

LENGTH OF PROGRAM: 2 hours

MATERIALS OR RESOURCES NEEDED

- Photo booth props
- Green screen (if no green screen, use a sheet)
- Cardboard to create a large frame
- Assorted costumes
- Wigs and wig caps
- Scarves, headbands, crowns, headbands
- Assorted accessories
- Optional: Hair and makeup volunteers

ACTIVITY

Creating a photo booth and then posing in it can be a lot of fun!

STEP 1. First you will need to set up an area where you either have a green screen or you can just make a large photo frame out of cardboard and attach it to a wall. You will also need to have a lot of props for the participants to wear, like wigs, scarves, funny headbands, ties, costume jewelry, and other accessories. Add some costumes that can be worn for the photos.

STEP 2. Break the group into teams of two and ask them to get ready for their photo opportunity. They can work in teams or if they feel more comfortable working on their own, they can do that too.

STEP 3. If you have hair and makeup volunteers, have them work with the teams or individuals and ask the latter to choose how they want their hair and makeup to look. This will be their chance to get their personal care on point, and there are so many things that they might need to do to get ready. Make a checklist for them to use when getting ready, and add on things like combing a mustache or beard. Also, make sure to smooth out wrinkles on outfits and check for color coordination.

STEP 4. There are many different levels of engagement that will come out of this activity, and all you need to take the photos is your smartphone or a digital camera. You can add additional fun to this activity by e-mailing everyone their photos so they can keep them as a memento and see how great they looked.

PHOTO BOOTH SUPERPOWERS

Prepare your students to . . .

- Prepare for a photo shoot.
- Use their personal care checklist.
- Dress for success.

9

Home Skills

Growing up, I have discovered over time, is rather like housework: never finished.
—LOIS MCMASTER BUJOLD

CLEANING THE HOUSE IS SOMETHING THAT EVERYONE NEEDS TO LEARN TO DO. To capture the essence of how to do household chores with your life skills program, it's important to cover every part of the house, from cleaning, vacuuming, disinfecting, and decluttering to home organization. The other important factor is that all of these must be done on a regular basis. Maintaining and managing a home comprise a very important life skills category. The ability to clean house is important, and you can teach these skills at the library with a variety of hands-on activities.

Mirrors and Magic

To clean or not to clean; that is the question. Well, that's a pretty easy question to answer. We all need to clean the house, but there are several answers to the question "why" and you can share this important message with your life skills participants. Cleaning up creates a pleasant place to reside and also improves the health and safety of those who live in the house. The best reason for cleaning, though, is because it feels amazing to have a clean, orderly space. This activity will encourage participants to practice cleaning and removing dirt and allergens, which will promote a healthier and happier living space for them.

LENGTH OF PROGRAM: 45 minutes

MATERIALS OR RESOURCES NEEDED

- Several hand mirrors
- White vinegar
- Dish soap
- Water
- Spray bottles
- Sponges
- Paper towels
- Soap or hair products (stuff to grime up the mirrors)

ACTIVITY

This is a fun activity to plan. All you need are several mirrors that can be purchased at a dollar or thrift store and some cleaners of your choice. Add in a bunch of sponges and some paper towels and that's it. A good idea for this activity is to use an environmentally friendly cleaner that is not toxic and doesn't have harsh fumes.

STEP 1. You can make a nontoxic cleaner by mixing one cup water, one cup vinegar, and a teaspoon of dishwashing liquid in a spray bottle. Shake it up and you're ready to go. The strategy for this activity is to get the mirrors dirty ahead of time. You can do this by splashing water on them. Dripping some soap or hair products on the glass and leaving them to dry on it will work great too.

STEP 2. When you're ready for the activity to start, let all the participants know that their job is to take a mirror and some cleaning supplies, along with sponges and paper towels. Explain to them that unfortunately bacteria can thrive on dirty surfaces for over a week. It's important to wipe down surfaces daily with bacteria-killing solutions like white vinegar. Give them a chance to work on cleaning their mirrors and ask them to pay special attention to the surfaces. It will be your job to inspect the mirrors to see if all of the smudges and grime have magically disappeared.

MIRROR CLEANING SUPERPOWERS

Prepare your students to . . .

- Learn about nontoxic cleaners.
- Take the time to clean up.
- Look for places where germs and bacteria hide.

Spring Cleaning Visualization

Back in the old days, spring cleaning was used to get rid of a winter's worth of smoke and soot generated by fireplaces, stoves, and furnaces when the warmer weather started in early spring. You can share this historical practice with your life skills participants and help them to understand the concept of spring cleaning. It's like a major overhaul to get rid of what you don't want or need anymore, reorganize your closets and living areas, and freshen up spaces for the year ahead. Planning a spring-cleaning activity will help your life skills program to learn about reorganizing and cleaning up spaces, which can have a totally energizing effect and can even spike productivity.

LENGTH OF PROGRAM: 1 hour

MATERIALS OR RESOURCES NEEDED

- 8½ × 11 paper
- Pens or pencils

ACTIVITY

This activity is a perfect way to introduce spring cleaning and to start a discussion about how nice it is to have a fresh new start.

STEP 1. At the start of this program, you may want to point out that doing a spring-cleaning overhaul can impart an invigorating and refreshing feeling. The idea is to clear everything you don't need out of a room, clean the room thoroughly, and then you will basically have a brand-new room. Sometimes it's hard to visualize what your house would look like if you did some major spring cleaning. This activity gives your life skills program the opportunity to do just that. Visualizing can also help to solidify what you need to do to make things happen in your life.

STEP 2. Let participants know that during spring cleaning they can even clean the carpet and paint the walls to give the room an extra fresh feeling. Ask everyone to get into small groups of about four or five. Then explain that each person should draw a picture of their house (or apartment) with all of the rooms inside of it. For example, 2 bedrooms, 1 bathroom, 1 kitchen, the living room, and perhaps a dining room. They can add all of the items that are currently in the rooms to their drawings. If they have a lot of clutter in the rooms, their house drawings will fill up fast.

STEP 3. Ask the groups to visualize what areas of their houses they would like to work on decluttering or cleaning up. Have each person draw another house with the same rooms, but with a new, decluttered look. After everyone is done, ask each participant to show their house drawings and talk about what it is like now and what they would like it to be like in the future. They can talk within their groups about what needs to be done and how they can accomplish the tasks. This activity will help them to visualize what they need to do and make it seem easier or more attainable. The activity can become the road map they need to start their spring cleaning, and cross off each room on their drawing after they're done.

SPRING CLEANING SUPERPOWERS
Prepare your students to . . .

- Declutter.
- Remove items they no longer need.
- Come up with cleaning strategies like cleaning one room at a time.
- Understand how clutter can cause negative health issues.

Safe Cleaning Solutions

Cleaning is very important in a home, and various cleaning supplies are essential for this. However, most cleaners in stores have chemicals that can be harmful and even dangerous. A great alternative for your life skills participants could be to make a safe household cleaner using a few basic items that can easily be found around the house. This activity offers an inventive way to try making different types of nontoxic cleaners that will also be much better for the environment.

LENGTH OF PROGRAM: 1 hour

MATERIALS OR RESOURCES NEEDED

- Supplies for experimental cleaners: baking soda, white vinegar, lemon juice, lemon peels, liquid dish soap, and salt
- Water (2 gallons)
- Box of regular tea bags
- Spray bottles (plastic or glass); at least 12 bottles
- Measuring cups (enough for four stations)
- Measuring spoons (enough for four stations)
- Tables
- Table covers to protect the tables
- Paper towels (for spills)
- Four small buckets or containers
- Hand mirrors (use the ones from the "Mirrors and Magic" activity)

ACTIVITY

This activity is set up so that your life skills program can make their own non-toxic cleaners and also take home what they make. There are many quick and simple recipes that will make excellent nontoxic or "green" cleaners.

STEP 1. You'll need some plastic spray bottles (these can also be empty bottles that have been repurposed). There are four different recipes for safe cleaners in this activity. Set up four stations—each station has one recipe and should include all the ingredients needed for that recipe. Make sure to cover each table and provide spray bottles, measuring cups, and paper towels at each station.

STEP 2. Let the group know that there are four different recipes to choose from. Ask them to take a look at each station and choose their favorite recipe. Once they have chosen, they can go to the station of their choice and take turns experimenting with the recipes there. This is a little like potions class in the Harry Potter series, so they may need to try a few times to get their concoctions right. You may want to have a small bucket at each station in case they need to start over again.

STEP 3. Let everyone try out their safe cleaners on the hand mirrors and use the paper towels to wipe them off. They should find that these cleaners work really well, and they also smell really nice.

ECO-FRIENDLY, NONTOXIC CLEANER RECIPES

SUPER CLEANER

Measure out ¼ cup of white distilled vinegar, 1 tablespoon of baking soda, 4 cups of water, and ½ cup of lemon juice and mix them together. Shake the spray bottle up and get ready to clean! This environmentally and safe cleaner will freshen up, scrub clean, and naturally disinfect all surfaces.

ZESTY LEMON CLEANER

Measure out ½ cup of lemon rinds, ¼ cup of white vinegar, 2 tablespoons of baking soda, and 4 cups of water and mix them together. Shake the spray bottle up for an extra good mixing. This spray is nontoxic and excellent for cleaning up and adds a fresh lemon smell.

FRAGRANT CLEANER

Measure out 1 cup of white vinegar, 1 cup of water, ½ cup of cut-up lemons, and 3 rosemary sprigs. Combine all of the ingredients together, pour into a spray bottle, and then shake vigorously. Use this all-star eco-friendly cleaner to remove stains, clean surfaces, and wipe away wall smudges. The fresh scent is invigorating, and the lemon boosts the cleaning power.

EASY BREEZY DUSTING SPRAY

Measure out 3 cups of water, add 2 tea bags, and 1 teaspoon of lemon juice. Shake well and spray on a paper towel. This nontoxic mixture can clean all of the dusty areas in the house.

NONTOXIC CLEANING SUPERPOWERS

Prepare your students to . . .

- Make their own nontoxic cleansers in order to cut down on packaging waste and reduce the release of chemicals into the air.
- Use natural, homemade cleaners to be safe.
- Practice green cleaning.
- Find items in the house to make a safe cleaner.

Couch Cushion Collage

Couches are notorious for sucking up all kinds of things, from coins to paper clips and other small items. Because it's easy to lose things under the couch cushions, it's important to include a life skills lesson on how to clean and declutter beneath the couch. Some of the most bizarre stories include someone finding a lizard skeleton and an old cigar! For this activity, we're going to dig deep into our craft shelves and office supplies to find items that fit the description of items you might find under the cushions, in order to plan a perfect demonstration for a life skills program.

LENGTH OF PROGRAM: 1 hour

MATERIALS OR RESOURCES NEEDED

- Small boxes (one per participant)
- Wide variety of craft supplies
- Cut-up pieces of paper
- Pennies
- Paper clips
- Hair clips
- Rubber bands
- Glue sticks
- Paper for collage work
- Tables and chairs

ACTIVITY

This is a fun way to show participants how to recycle or reuse their couch cushion collections.

STEP 1. The best way to prepare for this activity would be to visit your local dollar store and buy a lot of small things that look like they might be found under a couch cushion. You can use pennies, paper clips, ribbons, bows, hair clips, rubber bands, or even cut-up pieces of paper. Various other office supply items will work too.

STEP 2. Give each participant a small box with their couch cushion collection inside and ask them to make a collage. You can provide them with paper and glue and any other items they will need to create their collage. This activity is not so much a hands-on practice as it is an entertaining way to add in a craft project that the participants can take home. Craft sessions are also very soothing and relaxing and can promote mindfulness, so this activity has quite a few benefits.

COUCH CUSHION SUPERPOWERS

Prepare your students to . . .

- Check under the cushions regularly.
- Learn to declutter before things accumulate.
- Enjoy creating a colorful collage that promotes reusing and recycling materials.

Communication

Genius is the ability to put into effect what is on your mind.

—F. SCOTT FITZGERALD

COMMUNICATION IS A VERY IMPORTANT LIFE SKILL FOR ADULT SURVIVAL. IT'S a fact that texting—the sending of short electronic messages between two or more smartphones or other mobile devices—has affected how people communicate with each other. Today, texting has become a major form of communication for almost everyone. Because of this, life skills programs that focus on verbal or spoken communication and which help participants to relearn how to converse and collaborate with each other in person are extremely important. It is important because we will always use this basic type of communication at home, in our jobs, and wherever we go in the community—as well as when talking on our phones. Teaching about good verbal communication is crucial for your participants to build the skills needed to succeed in all aspects of their lives.

Connection Check-in

Communication is usually a two-way street, which means that one person speaks and the other one listens, and then vice versa. However, sometimes when someone is not listening or they're already thinking about what they're going to say, the lines of communication can become crossed. This activity will help your life skills participants to keep in mind that listening is about more than just hearing another person speak. To engage in effective communication, you must really focus on what the speaker is saying and understand or interpret what they really mean.

LENGTH OF PROGRAM: 30–45 minutes

MATERIALS OR RESOURCES NEEDED

- Chairs set in pairs

ACTIVITY

Listening helps you become more aware of your surroundings and also to learn something new. This is a very simple activity that has the power to activate strong listening skills.

STEP 1. To begin this activity, give participants a short overview and let them know that active listening is one of the key reasons why relationships become strong and solid. Everyone can listen, but not everyone can listen attentively and actively. This communication skill shows how sincere a person is and how they relate to the feeling or message that the speaker is sending. Be sure to let the group know that to engage in this active listening exercise, they will need to do these six things: be attentive, remain impartial, show empathy, interpret what was said, sum up the conversation, and make sure to participate equally.

STEP 2. After you have shared the six things, ask the group to pair up in twos to practice active listening. Ask each person to ask their partner how they're doing today and then listen without speaking while they share. Each person sharing will explain in a few sentences how they are doing. Then it will be their turn to ask how the other person is doing. After that, everyone in the program can share what they heard when their neighbor spoke to them. Communication involves connecting with people by actively listening and using your own voice. In a nutshell, it's about sending and receiving information and then processing this exchange of information. This activity is a great way to practice active listening.

ACTIVE LISTENING SUPERPOWERS

Prepare your students to . . .

- Listen actively and with intention.
- Have confidence when speaking.
- Be aware of nonverbal communication (body language).

Silence Is Golden

Everyone has their own quiet time or a time when they sit in silence and think. Often, however, when we're with someone else, we feel that we must talk because we don't want that awkward feeling when no one is talking. Teaching your life skills program about silence can help them to understand how this plays a part in communication and how it can be helpful. Understanding that silence can be a positive thing is an important communication skill. This activity focuses on silence as a tool that can further enhance communication.

LENGTH OF PROGRAM: 30 minutes

MATERIALS OR RESOURCES NEEDED

- Chairs set in pairs
- Timer

ACTIVITY

This activity can be a way to learn a higher level of communication. It can be somewhat uncomfortable, yet it can be extremely beneficial if you feel that you can't sit comfortably in silence with someone else. This is a great way to practice just sitting in silence and seeing how that feels.

STEP 1. Pair off participants into teams of two and have them sit facing each other. Explain to the groups that you're going to ask them to not speak at all once the activity starts. You might want to ask them if anyone has ever tried doing a staring contest, and there may be a few laughs.

STEP 2. Ask each team of two to stare into each other's eyes for as long as they can. The trick to this activity is to not say anything and to keep the eye connection going until the time is up. For the first round, set the timer for one minute and let them know that this was their practice time. Next round, set the timer for three minutes and the rules stay the same: no talking, just staring and making eye contact. Your job will be to see how many teams can stay silent and keep that eye connection going. The teams that make it to three minutes will be the champs. Ask the winners if they want to go for four minutes or more. You might have some takers, and the more they do this activity, the more confident they will feel in conversations and when silences occur.

The purpose of this activity is to give the group a chance to understand and honor the silence and space between two people. It is important to let them know that we don't always have to be talking and that silence doesn't have to be uncomfortable; it can actually be a positive experience and can bring about social awareness and accentuate communication skills.

SILENCE SUPERPOWERS
Prepare your students to . . .

- Move a conversation forward after silence.
- Understand the power of silence.
- Trust the reflective opportunities of silence.

 # Modeling through Movies

Do you love movies? That's great because you can use them to teach life skills programs about communication. Movies are actually one of the best ways to show what it's like to communicate with others, whether it be positive or negative. You can stop a movie, make a clip, and even rewind it so the group can take a closer look. Also, many movies portray social behavior and emotional states, so this makes them perfect for teaching a life skills program at the library.

LENGTH OF PROGRAM: 1 hour

MATERIALS OR RESOURCES NEEDED
- Laptop
- Projector
- Projector screen
- Six movie clips for effective communication
- Six movie clips for ineffective communication
- Tables and chairs

ACTIVITY

STEP 1. Start by finding about five or six movie clips, each around five minutes long, that model good or effective communication. Then find another five or six movie clips the same length as the others that model negative or ineffective communication. Try to mix them up and sequence clips that feature different ways of communicating. A few ideas for movie clips:

- Look for someone using both verbal and nonverbal language (body language), such as the tone and inflection of their voice, facial expression, bodily gestures, and eye gaze.
- Someone listening mindfully (or not). This means listening with their full attention and really trying to understand the speaker.
- Someone speaking with confidence in a clear and steady voice. They use eye contact and speak sincerely.
- Someone validating others and reflecting back by asking questions to clarify, so they show they are listening (and trying to understand).
- Someone apologizing. Saying you're sorry means you're taking responsibility for something or you're taking the blame for your actions.
- Someone asked to do something that goes against their own inclinations.
- Two people having a disagreement. Disagreements are okay when it comes to communicating as long as the people are polite and respectful to each other.

STEP 2. When everyone arrives for the program, explain that you will be showing movie clips, and at the end of each clip you would like everyone to share their opinions on whether the characters are displaying effective or ineffective communication. If you've already gone over this topic with the program, you can ask them to point out what type of communication the characters are exhibiting. Show the clips to the program participants one at a time, and don't give away the answer until everyone has had a chance to speak and explain what type of communication they think is being modeled. This will provide a lot of laughs and will be a great way for the group to understand and learn about effective and ineffective communication.

COMMUNICATION SUPERPOWERS
Prepare your students to . . .

- Be respectful when in a disagreement.
- Value the person who is speaking.
- Validate others by actively listening.

Drainpipe Challenge

Working in a team requires a lot of communication. The team has a goal to meet, and that takes patience, focus, and cooperation. Teaching your life skills program that effective communication allows everyone on the team to understand what needs to be done to achieve a goal can really enhance their knowledge. It also helps the team to create roles within their group in order to ensure that everyone on the team has a task and feels good about working together. This activity gives the participants hands-on practice for working in a team and achieving a common goal by communicating with each other.

LENGTH OF PROGRAM: 2 hours

MATERIALS OR RESOURCES NEEDED

- Recycled cardboard paper towel rolls (enough to make at least 6 cardboard drainpipes)
- Tape (packing, scotch, book, any kind of tape)
- Bag of marbles

ACTIVITY

Every team needs great communicators. Communication can help to prioritize the team's goals and keep everyone motivated. Communication, collaboration, and teamwork are what this activity is all about. Communicating in groups can help team members to develop a sense of belonging and strengthen their connections with other team members. Here's what you'll need to do for this goal-driven activity.

Divide the group into teams of two and give them each tools needed to build a drainpipe (paper towel rolls and tape) and a bunch of marbles. The goal for each team is for one member to figure out a way to send their marbles to the other team member. The trick is that only one of them can hold the drainpipe that they build, and they have to be at least three feet away from each other. Also, let them know that they can't throw the marbles at each other; that's not positive teamwork. The main rule is that they must use the drainpipe as a conduit to get the marbles to their team member. They can be as creative as possible.

The main purpose of this activity is to learn how to work together as a team and to find out how each individual contributes to the team. This activity will spur many different ways of communication that may or may not be effective. There will be a lot of innovative ideas, and teamwork and leadership skills will all be part of this activity. Try to save about 15 to 20 minutes after the challenge to have the groups get together and talk about their experience communicating in teams. Ask them to share what worked and what didn't. This will be an enlightening activity for everyone.

TEAMWORK SUPERPOWERS

Prepare your students to . . .

- Establish open communication within a team.
- Define clear roles and responsibilities for each team member.
- Utilize communication to accomplish a common goal.

11

Relationships
with Friends and Family

Relationships don't always make sense. Especially from the outside.
—SARAH DESSEN

RELATIONSHIPS ARE IMPORTANT AT ANY AGE. STABLE RELATIONSHIPS WITH family members, partners, and friends are especially important as they promote self-esteem and a strong sense of belonging. They can even influence our physical health. Teaching life skills participants about the value of relationships can also assist in their development of problem-solving and social skills. Those who are able to successfully establish and maintain positive relationships tend to be more satisfied with their lives and better adjusted well into later life. There are many activities that can enhance the skills needed to maintain healthy relationships. Look for activities that focus on honesty, trust, respect, and sharing.

Gift-Opening Challenge

Opening up to others is not always as easy as it seems. Sharing our feelings can make us feel awkward or uncomfortable and can even make us feel insecure. Teaching your life skills participants ways to open up and share their feelings can lead to mutual understanding and respect and can help them to value differences in views, interests, and needs. Being able to open up in conversations and maintain honest communication in any relationship is really important. This activity is perfect for practicing opening up and honestly sharing feelings in a safe and supportive setting.

LENGTH OF PROGRAM: 1 hour

MATERIALS OR RESOURCES NEEDED
- 20 candy bars or snack candies (or other small gifts)
- Large box
- Small pieces of paper (to use for wrapping the candy)
- List of engaging questions
- List of fun challenges

ACTIVITY

This activity will help to get your participants to open up on several different levels. The plan here is to have a box that has several layers of gifts that are wrapped in paper. You can start with a large box, and inside of that box will be around 20 small, wrapped gifts. The gifts can be something like a chocolate bar or a small bag of candy. The most important part of this activity is to include a question with each gift that, when answered, will reveal something about the person opening the gift. Think of questions that will not be too embarrassing, but that will reveal something you didn't know about the person answering them.

STEP 1. Have everyone in the group sit in a circle. Explain that the goal of this activity is to pass the gift box around the circle, and each person will get a turn to open a gift from the box. When they open it up there will be a question that they need to answer. Ask them to try to be open and honest and answer as best they can. There is also the option of taking a challenge if they don't want to answer the question.

STEP 2. To start this activity, give the first person the box of gifts and ask them to open one up. Then ask them to read their question out loud. Next, ask them if they want to answer the question or take the challenge. If they decide to take the challenge, have a list of challenges ready; these consist of asking them to do something funny like sing a song to the group, act out a scene from their favorite movie, or share their most embarrassing moment.

The best thing about this activity is that the group gets to snack on their prizes, learn more about each other, and have some good laughs as well. Be as creative as you want with the questions, and make the challenges as wacky as you want to get everyone talking.

IDEAS FOR QUESTIONS

- Who is your hero and why?
- What would you change about yourself if you could?
- What is your favorite book? Describe the characters.
- What makes you laugh, what do you think is funny, and why?
- If you could live or travel anywhere, where would it be?
- What's your favorite food, recipe, or meal, and why?
- Do you have a nickname? How did you get it?
- How would your family describe you? What are you really like?
- What are your hobbies?
- Do you have any pets? What are their names?

IDEAS FOR CHALLENGES

- Sing your favorite song to the group.
- Act out your favorite movie scene.
- Do ten jumping jacks.
- Ask the person next to you when their birthday is and what their favorite cake is.
- Act like a mime.
- Share your most embarrassing moment.
- Try to do a cheer or some dance moves.
- What's the funniest face you can make?
- Give us your best drumming performance.
- Do a cookie stacking challenge. How many cookies can you stack until they fall?

OPENING UP SUPERPOWERS

Prepare your students to . . .

- Be open and honest, which builds connections with others.
- Share their own personal stories.
- Laugh and have fun.

The Trust Obstacle Course

Trust is all about building connections and feeling safe with friends. One thing that happens when we are just starting out in a friendship is that we test the waters to see how it's going to go. Teaching your life skills participants that they might feel vulnerable or unsure when their trust is in the hands of someone else can be an extremely powerful experience. This activity is a way of getting to know what it's like to trust someone when you are going through the obstacles of life. The "obstacles" here might only be stuffed animals, but they still represent the vulnerability we manifest and the importance of trusting others when we need assistance and guidance.

LENGTH OF PROGRAM: 1 hour

MATERIALS OR RESOURCES NEEDED

- A variety of rubber cones
- Plastic bowling pins
- Stuffed animals in different sizes
- Toys (as many as you can find)

ACTIVITY

For this activity, you can use items like rubber cones, bowling pins, stuffed animals, toys, or anything else you have on hand.

STEP 1. Set up your obstacle course by placing all of the objects a short distance apart from each other. You can make them into a square, a circle, or any other configuration that forms an obstacle course. The best thing to do is to have the objects about one to two feet away from each other.

STEP 2. Divide the group into pairs. In each pair, one person will be blindfolded, and one will not have a blindfold. The team members will be on the opposite sides of the course from each other. Here's the fun part. The person who is not blindfolded will be the guide for the person that is blindfolded. The guide will be at the opposite end of the course and cannot enter the field. The guide must verbally direct the other team member through the obstacle course. This activity will be a fun and interesting test of listening skills and trust.

STEP 3. When you say "start," the guide will start calling out directions to the blindfolded person to help guide them through the obstacle course. The key to this activity is that the blindfolded person mustn't touch any of the objects (with feet or knees) or they will be out. If they move successfully through the course, the pair will then exchange roles, and the other member will try to get through the obstacle course safely. This activity helps create trust and respect for each other and also exemplifies how important listening skills are.

TRUST SUPERPOWERS

Prepare your students to . . .

- Follow through with their actions.
- Value the relationships they have.
- Build trust and earn the trust of others.

Circle of Respect

This activity is a perfect way to have life skills participants learn about respect and share their own thoughts and ideas in a safe space. Sometimes, understanding how a person is feeling is more important than what is actually being said. Being aware of what others are feeling is a great way to show respect and also to create connections and make friends.

LENGTH OF PROGRAM: 1 hour

MATERIALS OR RESOURCES NEEDED

- Prompts about respect

ACTIVITY

STEP 1. Have the participants sit in a circle all together. Once everyone is comfortable, introduce the concept of respect as part of a healthy relationship and ask them to say what they think respect means to them. Have each person contribute an idea about respect and what it means to them. For example, respectful behavior, talking about how it feels to be respected, how they show respect to friends and family, and how teachers show respect to students. If anyone is having trouble coming up with ideas, you may need to provide some prompts by asking questions about their background or experiences.

STEP 2. Have the group pair up into teams of two. Ask them to talk with each other about what respect means to them and how it applies to their life. They can talk about school, home, or their families and friends. Let them talk for about ten minutes and then bring the whole group back together. Wrap up the activity with a nice quote on respect like this one:

> Regard your good name as the richest jewel you can possibly be possessed of—for credit is like fire; when once you have kindled it you may easily preserve it, but if you once extinguish it, you will find it an arduous task to rekindle it again. The way to a good reputation is to endeavor to be what you desire to appear. —*Socrates*

PROMPTS FOR WHAT RESPECT MEANS

- What does respect mean to you?
- Describe a respectful person.
- Who do you know that has a lot of respect for others?
- Which animal is the most respectful?
- Have you heard the phrase "Have respect for your elders"? Why should we do this?
- Do you think respect is an important value?
- Should we respect the earth and the environment? How can we do this?
- Why do we have to respect rules or laws?

RESPECT SUPERPOWERS

Prepare your students to . . .

- Value patience and respect.
- Understand and nurture trust.
- Treat everyone with respect.

Putting the Pieces Together

This activity models the concepts of how we fit together and how we get along with others. It teaches life skills participants about relationships, collaboration, and finding common goals. Some people feel that navigating relationships is like solving a jigsaw puzzle. This is a pretty good analogy; relationships have no real starting point and sometimes can feel disconnected. They can be complex, and there are no real instructions. This activity proves that putting the pieces of a puzzle together works a lot better when you have others to collaborate with. It also highlights how cooperation works in relationships.

LENGTH OF PROGRAM: 1 hour

MATERIALS OR RESOURCES NEEDED

- Puzzle pieces (1 puzzle box per group will work)
- Tables and chairs

ACTIVITY

STEP 1. Find several small puzzles with all of the pieces in the box. Fitting the pieces together is what is going to make this activity a successful one. Put a puzzle box on each table and wait for participants to get settled.

STEP 2. Create a few small groups with 4 or 5 team members each and give each group a box of puzzle pieces. Give them the task of working together to put the puzzle pieces together and give them about 45 minutes to work on this project.

STEP 3. Check in with each group to see how their progress is coming. Did they work together successfully and put their puzzle together, or did they have a hard time working together? Did one person take over, or did they all work together? Have each group share about their experience putting the puzzle pieces together. Ask them to describe how they worked together as a group and if they enjoyed the experience.

COOPERATION AND COLLABORATION SUPERPOWERS

Prepare your students to . . .

- Cooperate and get things done.
- Problem-solve with friends.
- Collaborate, create, and build new relationships.

12

Stress Management

We must have a pie. Stress cannot exist in the presence of a pie.

—DAVID MAMET

STRESS MANAGEMENT STRATEGIES ARE AN IMPORTANT PART OF LIFE SKILLS. Teaching life skills students how to understand and manage stress can be very helpful for them. Utilizing resources and stress management techniques can help them to de-stress. We can also teach them that in some situations, stress acts as an alarm system that kicks into gear when we need it most. Stress is most harmful when it is continuous and there is nothing that can relieve it. If the tension becomes too excessive, it can set off an array of endless challenges. The activities in this chapter can help to alleviate stress and are great for managing stress.

Dance Party Zone

Have you heard of the saying "You've gotta dance like there's nobody watching" by William W. Purkey? Well, he's right! Dancing is a great way to let loose, and it also relieves stress. Get your life skills participants out on the dance floor and get them ready to boogie. The most wonderful thing about dancing is that they don't even have to know how to dance; it's all free-flowing at a dance party. When they start dancing, there's nothing to think about; just listen to the music and groove to the beat. Dancing like no one is watching is also a great way to express yourself.

LENGTH OF PROGRAM: 1–2 hours

MATERIALS OR RESOURCES NEEDED

- Large space with room for dancing
- Bluetooth speaker or karaoke machine
- Refreshments: water, punch, small snacks (chips, crackers, popcorn)
- Table for refreshments
- A few chairs

ACTIVITY

A dance party is an excellent event to host for your life skills program. Not only is it super fun, but it also gives a hands-on example of how physical movement is beneficial for stress management. This is a great idea, especially at those times of year when everyone gets really stressed, like tax time, final exams, the holidays, and so on. If you've been working with the same group on a series of programs, you could invite everyone to make a list of their five favorite dance songs ahead of time and then play them at the dance party.

STEP 1. The best way to set up a dance party at the library is to plan ahead. First, come up with a name or theme for your event. You could call it something like "Dance Away the Blues" and ask everyone to come dressed in blue. Or you might want to call it something like "Stress Away Island," go with a tropical theme, and give out flower leis when everyone arrives. Once you've found the name for your event, make sure to have a flyer or invitation so that everyone will know when and where the event will be. You'll also need to find a space big enough for a group to dance in. And then you must make sure to have some awesome music. If you happen to have some funds, you could get a DJ. However, you don't really need one if you have a phone and Bluetooth. There are several portable Bluetooth speakers with party effects and flashing lights that will play the music loud enough for everyone to dance to. If you make the playlist ahead of time, there will be nonstop music unless everyone decides to take a break. Another idea would be to have a library staff member help with the music, so you are free to mingle with the group and practice your own dance moves.

STEP 2. Refreshments are a must when having a dance party. After moving and grooving for a long time, everyone will be thirsty and might want a snack or two for more energy. The best idea for drinks would be to make a punch. One of the best punch recipes out there is lemon-lime soda, pineapple juice, and lemonade all mixed together. You can also add some sherbet ice cream for a lovely color and taste. The snacks should be simple, like a variety of potato chips, crackers, and popcorn. Mini cupcakes are always a big hit, and of course any snacks that go with your theme are a good idea.

STEP 3. For this part it's all about dancing to the music. Just let the group go with the flow and see how they enjoy the mood-boosting benefits of the physical activity. There are many more benefits from dancing. It can help you think more clearly, lower blood pressure, and improve confidence. I think it goes without saying that William W. Purkey knew a little something about the benefits of dancing and the power it holds to help us step out of our comfort zone and let go of any pressures or tensions in our lives.

LEMONY LIME FRUIT PUNCH RECIPE

- 1 liter of lemon-lime soda
- 1 12 oz. can of pineapple juice
- 1 12 oz. can of frozen lemonade concentrate
- Any flavor of sherbet ice cream

Mix all of the ingredients in a very large punch bowl. Pour the punch into cups and add one scoop of sherbet on top. Delicious!

DANCE FLOOR SUPERPOWERS

Prepare your students to . . .

- Find ways to relieve stress by dancing.
- Express their emotions and promote creativity.
- Stay active and enjoy the positive energy on the dance floor.

Take Your Mind on a Walk

Mindfulness is the practice of paying full attention to the present moment, of being fully present and aware of ourselves, our actions, and our surroundings. When you're mindful, you are more intensely aware of what you are feeling, so practicing mindfulness routinely is a great way to reduce stress. With this activity, you can teach your life skills participants to go even deeper with mindfulness. Let them take a few minutes to practice being with their thoughts. This really helps them to feel what it's like to be in the moment. This activity is perfect for a life skills program because it focuses on physicality and mindfulness. You could also help the group to develop a mantra that they will repeat in their thoughts as they take their mind on a walk.

LENGTH OF PROGRAM: 1 hour

MATERIALS OR RESOURCES NEEDED

- Large space big enough for the group to spread out

ACTIVITY

Mindfulness is like taking a short vacation in your mind. This activity is perfect for when you can't take participants outside and you really want to incorporate a stress relief activity for your program. Mindful walking is brilliant because it combines the benefits of exercise and mindfulness.

STEP 1. Ask participants to spread out in the room and get enough space where they can move freely. Then let them know that they will be walking in place. Ask them to concentrate on the movement of their walking and try to clear their minds. However, you really want them to anchor themselves in the present. They can continually keep walking in place at whatever speed works for them.

STEP 2. Have the group do this for about fifteen minutes and then stop for a break. If they get tired, they can stop and rest in place and restart their walking movements again. Try for another fifteen minutes and then stop and have everyone join back together in a circle. Go round the group and ask everyone to say how they feel after their mind-walking adventure. They should feel excited or exhilarated by this mindfulness-and-movement activity, and the great thing is that they can do this activity at home or anywhere else that works for them.

MIND WALKING SUPERPOWERS

Prepare your students to . . .

- Imagine themselves in a happy place.
- Feel more in the zone.
- Find more enhanced concentration.

Positivity Manifestation Board

Positive thinking has a lot of power when working with life skills programs. The beauty of positive thinking is that it can make problems seem more manageable, and it helps to approach difficult situations in a more fruitful way. Practicing positivity will allow your life skills program participants to adapt easier and will promote resiliency. Those who are positive or optimistic can also inspire others. The thing about positivity is that the more positive you are, the more positivity you will receive back. This activity is a tribute to positive thinkers everywhere. Your participants will truly be inspired!

LENGTH OF PROGRAM: 1 hour

MATERIALS OR RESOURCES NEEDED

- Poster boards
- Magazines
- Glue
- Tape
- Scissors
- Embellishments like ribbons, fabric scraps, buttons
- Glitter
- Assorted recycled craft materials
- Tables and table covers (this could get messy)
- Chairs

ACTIVITY

This activity is an excellent way to tie together stress management and positivity. All you need for this activity are poster boards, magazines, glue or tape, and other embellishments like ribbon or glitter. Who doesn't love glitter? It would also be good if you could make this a sustainable project and use recycled craft materials. What a great way to do a positive thing for the planet!

STEP 1. Ask your participants to look through the magazines and cut out pictures that they think are positive or which make them happy to look at. Ask them to use all of the materials you have provided, along with the magazine cutouts, to create a manifestation board that focuses on being positive and stress-free.

STEP 2. Give them some time to work on their boards. You can walk around and ask them how their positivity board is going. Let them express how they're feeling while working on their project. They will have a great time adding their images, and they can take them home and keep adding to their board as time goes on.

VISION BOARD SUPERPOWERS

Prepare your students to . . .

- Reduce stress and unwind.
- Focus on positivity and on personal goals.
- Visualize positive changes and feel empowered.

 ## Prioritize This!

Time management isn't easy. From the moment we get up in the morning and start our day we are subject to a million things that attract our attention, and this can cause many of us to stress. You can teach your life skills participants about time management and how the role it plays in creating stress is very important. This activity can help participants to understand how to compartmentalize tasks and prioritize what needs to get done. Time management can save a lot of time and also take away any worry that comes from feeling overwhelmed.

LENGTH OF PROGRAM: 1 hour

MATERIALS OR RESOURCES NEEDED

- Tables and chairs
- Paper
- Pens and pencils
- Variety of office supplies (if needed)
- List of tasks (enough for 45 minutes)

ACTIVITY

Having a job can keep you very busy, and this can sometimes get overwhelming when there are too many tasks to do. That's why time management and prioritizing tasks are very important elements that will keep us on track. When we have too many tasks and not enough time, we can get overwhelmed, and that's when the stress takes over. This activity gives participants a chance to practice tasks in order of their importance while working within a limited time frame. It is a fun and playful way to practice time management skills, which will essentially help to reduce stress.

STEP 1. To start, you will need to make a list of tasks that you want the groups to do. Make sure to give a point value for each task; for example, introducing yourself is worth 5 points. Make the tasks fairly simple, such as the following ones: give each member of the group a nickname, tell the group something special about yourself, gather as many pencils as you can and bring them to your group, pitch a fun work idea you have to your group, do a crazy dance and get your teammates to do it too, sprint from one end of the room to the other, and so on. Just make sure that you list enough tasks that will take the participants at least 45 minutes or a little more, just in case.

STEP 2. Break participants into smaller groups of 4 or 5 team members. Hand out the lists to each of the groups. Let them know they need to decide which tasks to complete first, and they can decide what each team member's role will be on the team. Let the teams know they have about 45 minutes to complete all of the tasks on their list.

STEP 3. Watch as they try to prioritize and go through their lists; this will be a fun activity for everyone. Allow for about 15 minutes after the activity to talk about how they felt about the activity and how they decided on which tasks to complete first. You can have each group tally up how many tasks they completed and how many points they received. The group with the highest points can be declared the winner. While this activity is good for understanding how we can get stressed from too many tasks, it also helps to teach about group dynamics and how that relates to the workplace.

Each team member introduces themselves	5 points
Give your team a name	5 points
Tell the group something special about yourself	5 points
Gather as many pencils as you can	5 points
One team member does a dance and gets teammates to do it	10 points
All team members sprint from one end of the room to the other	15 points
Three team members pitch a fun work idea	10 points

TIME MANAGEMENT SUPERPOWERS

Prepare your students to . . .

- Avoid the urge to multitask.
- Take breaks.
- Manage their time carefully and stay organized.

Conclusion
Taking Care of Business

AS YOU CAN SEE, A LOT GOES INTO CREATING LIFE SKILLS PROGRAMS AT THE library. But even with all the planning, partnering, and promotions that are involved, the benefits of these programs can be immense. In most cases, once you start your life skills programs, you will continue to offer them on a regular basis. The nice thing is that once you have gone through the entire process of creating a life skills program, you can save yourself some time by duplicating many elements from program to program as you go. You can use the same planning template and go through the same steps with each topic that you feel is relevant for your program.

With minor edits, you may be able to use the same marketing and promotion tools for each program. Often, you can use the same materials and flyers if you just change the topic and the description. You will be saving time and creating a unified program—and this consistent approach will help the entire series to flow together.

You can easily plan at least six months ahead just by covering the topics we have gone over in this book. If you are daring, you can even plan a whole year of life skills programs. You can start anytime of the year.

So where do we go from here? This is where you begin planning your own life skills program and, most importantly, creating the content or curriculum that will hit it right out of the park.

Learning important life skills can be a great experience for participants, and it will help them to try and learn new things. In turn, trying something new will strengthen their confidence. This will allow them to grow and move forward, which supports being prepared in adulthood. Remember: it takes time to learn all of the different life skills and there will be trial and error, and of course there is always Google and YouTube to use for learning the skills, but we know that people will learn a lot more at a library life skills program. Most importantly, providing hands-on learning can really make a difference by providing a deeper understanding and a more meaningful experience.

Just remember to let your participants know that they are doing fine, and they will be ready in their own time.

Planning Template
for a Life Skills Program

PROGRAM TITLE

Come up with a catchy title for your class—one that makes it clear what the topic is, but which also appeals to your target audience.

PROGRAM DESCRIPTION

Write a thorough description of the program. Include the date, time, length, and the topic (or topics) that will be covered.

GOALS AND OBJECTIVES
What will participants be able to do as a result of participating in the class?
What knowledge, skills, awareness, or abilities will they gain?

_____

_____

_____

_____

_____

TOPICS TO BE COVERED
What life skills knowledge will be introduced in the session?

_____

_____

_____

_____

_____

ACTIVITIES
How will you make the session hands-on and interactive? What activities will
help participants practice and apply the learning?

_____

_____

_____

_____

PRESENTERS

Who will present the class? Include that person's name, title, and contact information.

_____

_____

PARTNERS

Who are your partners for the class? And what role will they play? Will they provide resources (brochures, etc.)? Will they attend the session? Will they help market the session?

_____

_____

MARKETING

How will you get the word out about the class? What, when, and where will you promote the program in order to reach your target audience?

_____

_____

_____

EVALUATION

How will you measure the success of the class? Will you create a survey for participants to take after the session? If so, what questions will you include?

_____

_____

_____

_____

_____

Reading Tie-Ins

INTRODUCTION: YOU'VE GOT THIS!

The Craft of Librarian Instruction by Julie Artman, Jeff Sundquist, and Douglas R. Dechow. American Library Association, 2016.

> This book is a must-have for any librarian embarking on the journey of teaching at the library. The authors compare teaching to that of performing in a theatrical performance and offer many different tips and techniques. Their main points are rehearsing, preparing, connecting with participants through role-playing, and sharpening your teaching presence. These are all excellent tips, and this book is very helpful if you have experienced shyness when the spotlight is on you.

The Destiny Formula: Find Your Purpose, Overcome Your Fear of Failure, Use Your Natural Talents and Strengths to Build a Successful Life by Ayodeji Awosika. CreateSpace, 2016.

> This book is all about planning and having a purpose in life. It is filled with positive notions on how to become ambitious and how to make something out of nothing. This book is for people who know deep down they could be doing more and need some strategies to get to where they truly want to be. This is a perfect book to offer to life skills participants to help them find their purpose in life.

The Defining Decade: Why Your Twenties Matter and How to Make the Most of Them Now by Dr. Meg Jay. Twelve, 2013.

People have said that age is not a number and that it can't be defined. They have also said that becoming an adult is something that you can put off indefinitely or at least until you're forty-something, right? Well, this theory might not be true. Dr. Meg Jay, a clinical psychologist, argues that being in your twenties has been minimized and downplayed over the past few decades. Because of this, many people aren't even trying to transition into adulthood. Dr. Jay has a lot to say about the defining decade of adulthood. This book is for anyone looking for tips on relationships, personality, social networks, or identity and would be helpful when planning a life skills program.

CHAPTER 1: LET'S START PLANNING

The Useful Book: 201 Life Skills They Used to Teach in Home Ec and Shop by Sharon Bowers and David Bowers. Workman, 2016.

This book is extremely useful. It offers illustrated step-by-step instructions for any kind of project you can think of. You can find DIY projects, fix-it help, cleaning ideas, cooking how-to instructions, and more. There are 201 practical projects listed, all with easy-to-follow instructions. This book is the go-to source for any life skills planning.

Presence: Bringing Your Boldest Self to Your Biggest Challenges by Amy Cuddy. Little, Brown, 2015.

Let's talk about personal power and how to strengthen your own personal presence. Personal power is important and many people don't know how to harness their own power, which may make them unable to meet the challenges they face in their lives. Whether it's a job interview, or dealing with conflict, or anything outside our comfort zone, we tend to look at it with dread, and this can often make us feel powerless. Gaining personal power can be a game changer, and this book is a must-read for anyone who is looking for inspiration.

Library Conversations: Reclaiming Interpersonal Communication Theory for Understanding Professional Encounters by Marie L. Radford and Gary P. Radford. ALA Neal-Schuman, 2017.

> Focusing on communication and being present in day-to-day interactions is very important for all of us. It is also important to remember that interpersonal skills are just as valuable as life skills, and this book touches on the theory, research, and models of success that can be incorporated into first-rate communication practices.

CHAPTER 2: PARTNERSHIP OPPORTUNITIES AND PROGRAM PROMOTIONS

Library Collaborations and Community Partnerships: Enhancing Health and Quality of Life, edited by Vicki Hines-Martin, Fannie M. Cox, and Henry R. Cunningham. Routledge, 2020.

> If you're looking for information or ideas on how to collaborate, then this is the book for you. You will find key principles on how to create community partnerships and thus stay engaged with your community. The book offers excellent resources and information as well as strategies, challenges, outcomes, and lessons. This could provide a great start in finding partners for your life skills programs.

Crash Course in Marketing for Libraries, 2nd edition, by Susan W. Alman and Sara Gillespie Swanson. ABC-CLIO, 2014.

> This fantastic book is a treasure chest full of marketing ideas that you can utilize when promoting life skills programs at your library. Take a look at this book before you do your marketing and promotions because it provides some very powerful tools.

CHAPTER 3: EVALUATE AND SUSTAIN YOUR LIFE SKILLS PROGRAMS

Five Steps of Outcome-Based Planning and Evaluation for Public Libraries by Melissa Gross, Cindy Mediavilla, and Virginia A. Walter. American Library Association, 2016.

> If you're new to working on outcomes and evaluations, then this is the book for you. There's something for everyone here, including the

elements of planning and evaluating with a holistic approach. You'll find tips on how to create services that are targeted to your particular community and on how to attain the outcomes that are your program's goals. The book also provides examples of how to easily manage the outcome and evaluation process.

Advancing a Culture of Creativity in Libraries: Programming and Engagement by Megan Lotts. American Library Association, 2021.

This book emphasizes how important it is to nurture creativity and offer hands-on instruction in engaging learning events that build trust and foster well-being. Author Megan Lotts shows how libraries can encourage their staff to look at teaching and learning in a more interactive way. The book includes real case studies of libraries that have taken on creative projects, and also has an important section on learning from setbacks and failure.

CHAPTER 4: JOBS

What Color Is Your Parachute? 2021: Your Guide to a Lifetime of Meaningful Work and Career Success by Richard N. Bolles and Katharine Brooks. Ten Speed, 2020.

I remember reading What Color Is Your Parachute? when I was searching for what to do in my life. I was trying to figure out what kind of job I should get, and I found the book to be quite inspiring. This newest version of it does not disappoint. There is ageless advice, incredible insights, and relevant perspectives on today's job market and what it takes to make it in the world of work. This book is for anyone who is new at job searching and finding the right career for themselves.

Becoming the Boss: New Rules for the Next Generation of Leaders by Lindsey Pollak. HarperBusiness, 2014.

This is an inspiring book that can help support a new generation of managers. It offers the latest and most applicable ideas on career success. The book explains how Millennials will be moving up into positions of leadership when the older generations step down. The way that Pollak approaches the idea of Millennials moving into leadership is engaging and helps us to understand the motivations and understanding of this particular generation.

Finding Your Own North Star: Claiming the Life You Were Meant to Live by
Martha Beck. Harmony, 2002.

> Author Martha Beck has created a book that helps you to find your own
> internal compass. Her book is about tapping into your own consciousness
> and targeting what your blocks in life are. Beck includes case studies,
> questionnaires, and simple exercises to help focus on what motivates
> and inspires you. This book is a true gem and is helpful for pursuing your
> ambitions and dreams in both your career and your life.

CHAPTER 5: MONEY

*Why Didn't They Teach Me This in School? 99 Personal Money Management
Principles to Live By* by Cary Siegel. CreateSpace, 2013.

> Siegel's book is packed full of great tips and advice for anyone who is new
> at money management and would be an excellent guide for planning
> activities and lessons for life skills programs that focus on money. The
> topics include how to budget, ideas for investing money, how to approach
> your first job, and how to save money to move out on your own. The book
> is a quick read and could be added to your life skills library to have on
> hand for program participants to read. Siegel's sound advice comes from
> his own real-life experiences.

Get Good with Money: Ten Simple Steps to Becoming Financially Whole by
Tiffany Aliche. Rodale Books, 2021.

> *Get Good with Money* explains how to achieve financial security by saving
> money with a practical and feasible money management system. The
> book offers supportive checklists, interactive worksheets, and an impres-
> sive toolkit with ample resources. Aliche uses simple techniques and
> includes both baseline budgeting tips and detailed steps to take action on
> managing your money.

CHAPTER 6: COOKING

How to Cook Everything: Simple Recipes for Great Food by Mark Bittman.
Harvest, 2019.

> You need a good cookbook with simple recipes if you're a starter cook like
> me. This book fits the bill and is filled with recipes galore. You will find

non-stressful and to-the-point recipes, with easy-to-read instructions for basic cooking any time of the year.

Prep School: How to Improve Your Kitchen Skills and Cooking Techniques by James P. DeWan. Agate Surrey, 2016.

You will definitely want to include this book in your life skills collection. James P. DeWan is a culinary instructor and award-winning food writer, and his work comes to life in this book. Prep School is a perfect read for anyone who wants to learn how to become a better cook and is searching for the perfect techniques. The full-color photography throughout the book makes this a trusty guide for beginner cooks.

CHAPTER 7: SELF-CARE

The Self-Care Solution: A Year of Becoming Happier, Healthier, and Fitter— One Month at a Time by Jennifer Ashton. William Morrow, 2019.

Dr. Jennifer Ashton is an award-winning chief medical correspondent for *ABC News* and *Good Morning America*. In this book she provides her expertise on self-care with a month-to-month focus on the struggles she has faced and how she overcame difficult challenges. Ashton includes monthly lessons in an easy-to-understand format. Included in the book are inspirational tips and ideas on how to incorporate self-care into your lifestyle.

The No Worries Workbook: 124 Lists, Activities, and Prompts to Get Out of Your Head—and On with Your Life! by Molly Burford. Adams Media, 2019.

Author Molly Burford has come up with a great book that focuses on how we can worry less and take better care of ourselves. This workbook or guide includes many goodies that can be used in your life skills programs. From creative activities, quotes, and journal prompts to light cognitive exercises, you get all the pointers you need to create a vital program or workshop on self-care.

CHAPTER 8: PERSONAL CARE

How to Get Dressed: A Costume Designer's Secrets for Making Your Clothes Look, Fit, and Feel Amazing by Alison Freer. Ten Speed, 2015.

Alison Freer is a costume designer who has created a book full of amazing tips on how to dress for any occasion. This is the perfect guide for anyone who needs to learn how to dress for success, and Freer's pointers can help when creating a new wardrobe. This would be an excellent book for your life skills collection.

Laundry Love: Finding Joy in a Common Chore by Patric Richardson and Karin B. Miller. Flatiron Books, 2021.

Author Patric Richardson knows all about laundry; he runs a laundry camp where he teaches learners how to tackle sorting lights and darks and deciphering wash cycles. The book also covers how to deal with dry cleaning, ironing, and getting stains out of clothing. This is a comprehensive guide that will make a great companion for a life skills program that focuses on personal care.

Skincare: The Ultimate No-Nonsense Guide by Caroline Hirons. HQ, 2020.

Caroline Hirons has been dubbed the skin care queen because of her blog and YouTube channel, which has over 100 million viewers. This book is helpful for people of all ages and explains the differences in skin types and how to properly take care of your skin. Hirons gives tips on how to have good skin and also debunks myths about skin care. There is also information on how to read the ingredients in skin care products.

CHAPTER 9: HOME SKILLS

A Monk's Guide to a Clean House and Mind by Shoukei Matsumoto. Particular Books, 2018.

This house cleaning guide is very impressive. Matsumoto is a Buddhist monk who knows a thing or two about finding enlightenment. He shares his thoughts on how simple acts of daily cleaning can reduce clutter and create a calm atmosphere. The idea is that if you make your home cleaner and more tranquil, you will feel energized and content.

Life Skills: How to Cook, Clean, Manage Money, Fix Your Car, Perform CPR, and Everything in Between by Julia Laflin. Racehorse, 2020.

Author Julia Laflin has come up with a complete guide on life skills and includes a lot of information on how to build practical skills. This book is complete with all the essential things we need to know in order to cook, clean, manage money, and do many other things. This book is a must for your life skills collection. In it you will find many ideas for activities and content for your life skills programs.

CHAPTER 10: COMMUNICATION

Active Listening Techniques: 30 Practical Tools to Hone Your Communication Skills by Nixaly Leonardo. Rockridge, 2020.

Active listening is a very important aspect of communication. Nixaly Leonardo has come up with a book that covers excellent practice skills and techniques for sharpening how you listen to others. These tools can be applied to your life skills workshops and would be perfect to add to your program collection to help participants learn and practice their communication skills.

Communication Skills: Your Guide to Improving Social Intelligence, Developing Charisma, and Learning How to Talk to Anyone by Devin White. More Books, 2021.

Communication is the key to talking to other people, and this book hits the mark by targeting the most important factors of communication in today's world. Author Devin White explains how to become an amazing communicator and a compelling listener. The book offers a list of activities to try to practice communication skills. Strategies in the book also help to improve social intelligence and remove communication barriers.

CHAPTER 11: RELATIONSHIPS WITH FRIENDS AND FAMILY

The Friendship Formula: How to Say Goodbye to Loneliness and Discover Deeper Connection by Kyler Shumway. Kyler Shumway, 2018.

Friendship Formula is well written and easy to follow. Author Kyler Shumway has designed the book to provide interactive lessons and Q&A in each chapter. What is most helpful in this book is that it grabs your interest right away, helps you to think about friendship, and helps you to understand how friendships and relationships work. Friendship involves give-and-take, and this book offers a way to learn how to make a friend and keep that friendship going.

We Should Get Together: The Secret to Cultivating Better Friendships by Kat Vellos. Kat Vellos, 2020.

Making friends is not always as easy as it sounds. The art of friendship comes from learning how to talk and to listen to someone and to practice compassion and understanding. This book by Kat Velos is a handbook on how to make friends with people. She covers the common challenges when it comes to making friends and then gives an extensive guide on how to make and maintain friends for life. Included are practical tips, amazing relatable stories, and 300 conversation starters. This is one book that you will want to add to your life skills collection, in order to take your program on friendships to the next level.

CHAPTER 12: STRESS MANAGEMENT

Burnout: The Secret to Unlocking the Stress Cycle by Emily Nagoski and Amelia Nagoski. Ballantine Books, 2019.

This book is all about ending the cycle that stress creates. Those feelings of being overworked and overwhelmed can't be ignored; instead we should try and understand how we can remove some of the obstacles in our lives that are causing the stress. Sisters Emily and Amelia Nagoski have worked together on this book to create helpful strategies to combat stress and help turn it off and prevent burnout. There are helpful worksheets and exercises that can be used in a life skills program that focuses on stress management. There is also some very helpful advice from the authors.

Nature and Virtue Themed Exercises for Relaxation and Concentration: Guided Imagery, Visualizations, and Drawing Tasks by Maria Murto and Päivi Halmekoski. Deltaspektri, 2021.

This book is great for leading a guided imagery session with your program and can help create harmony between the mind and body. Guided imagery is a way of focusing and using your imagination to create calm, peaceful images in the mind, thereby providing an escape from stress. In this book there are many examples of exercises that can be done indoors or outdoors, and all have easy instructions on how to work in a group setting.

Index

A
active listening, 71–72
audience, target age group for, 14

B
benchmarks, 18
budget planning, 33–37

C
careers. *See* jobs/careers
charades, personal care, 55–57
cleaning solutions, 66–68
communication
　listening skills, 71–72
　movies, teaching using, 74–75
　silence, 73–74
　teamwork, 76–77
　See also relationships
cooking
　grocery shopping, 39–41
　importance of as topic, 5
　meal planning, 41–42
　pizza, 43–46
　smoothies, 42–43
cooperation/collaboration, 85–86
couches, cleaning, 69–70
creative outlets, 49–50
criteria for evaluation, 18

D
dancing, 87–89
dental care, 57–58
dogs, 53–54

E
Easy Breezy Dusting Spray, 68
eco-friendly cleaners, 68
evaluation of program, 17–18

F
Facebook, 14–15
family. *See* communication; relationships

feelings, sharing, 79–81
financial literacy jeopardy, 34–35. *See also* money management
Fragrant Cleaner, 68
friends. *See* communication; relationships

G
goals, setting, 4
grocery shopping, 39–41

H
hands-on learning
　ideas for, 6
　value of, 6
handwritten notes, 28–30
home skills
　cleaning solutions, 66–68
　couches, cleaning, 69–70
　mirror cleaning, 60–61
　spring cleaning, 65–66
hosts, 4–5

I
interviews
　communication after, 28–30
　mock, 26–28
　preparing for, 25–26

J
jobs/careers
　application process, 23–24
　importance of as topic, 5
　interview prep skills, 25–26
　mock job interviews, 26–28
　search process, 25–26
　thank-you notes, 28–30

L
Lemony Lime Fruit Punch recipe, 89
life skills programs
　communication, 71–77
　conclusion regarding, 95–96

life skills programs *(cont'd)*
    cooking, 39–46
    evaluation of, 17–18
    home skills, 63–70
    importance of, xv–xvi
    jobs/careers, 23–30
    money management, 31–37
    partnerships for, 11–13
    personal care, 55–61
    planning, 3–9
    promotions for, 13–15
    relationships, 79–86
    self-care, 47–54
    stress management, 87–94
    sustaining, 18–19
    template for, 7–9, 97–99
    timing of, 18–19
listening skills, 71–72

M

marketing, 13–15
meal planning, 41–42
mindfulness, 90–91
mirror cleaning, 63–64
mock job interviews, 26–28
money management
    financial literacy, 34–35
    importance of as topic, 5
    needs vs. wants, 33–34
    teaching importance of, 23–24
    travel, 35–37
movies, teaching communication using,
    74–75

N

needs vs. wants, 33–34
nontoxic cleaner recipes, 68
nutrition. *See* cooking; meal planning

O

objectives, setting, 4
online job applications, 23–24
opening up/sharing, 79–81

P

packing a suitcase, 58–59
partnership opportunities, 11–12
personal care
    charades for, 55–57
    dental care, 57–58
    packing a suitcase, 58–59
    photo booth activity for, 60–61
pets, 53–54

photo booth activity for personal care,
    60–61
pizza, learning to cook, 43–46
positive thinking, 91–92
practice interviews, 26–28
presenters, 4–5, 12–13
program design, overview of, 6
promotions, 13–15

R

Random Acts of Kindness (RAKs), 51–52
relationships
    cooperation/collaboration, 85–86
    opening up/sharing, 79–81
    respect, 83–84
    trust, 82–83
    See also communication
respect, 83–84

S

self-care
    creative outlets, 49–50
    pets, 53–54
    Random Acts of Kindness (RAKs),
        51–52
    teaching importance of, 47–49
silence, 73–74
smoothies, learning to make, 42–43
social media, 14–15
spring cleaning, 65–66
stress management
    dancing, 87–89
    mindfulness, 90–91
    positive thinking, 91–92
    time management, 92–94
suitcase, packing, 58–59
Super Cleaner, 68
sustaining program, 17–18

T

teamwork, 76–77
teeth/dental care, 57–58
thank-you notes, 28–30
time management, 92–94
topics, choosing, 5
traveling, 35–37, 58–59
trust, 82–83

W

wants, needs vs., 33–34

Z

Zesty Lemon Cleaner, 68